# ROOM AT THE INN

*Love Checks Into Two Christmas Novellas*

## KRISTY DYKES
## PAMELA GRIFFIN

BARBOUR
PUBLISHING

Published by Barbour Publishing, Inc., P.O. Box 719, Uhrichsville, Ohio 44683 www.barbourbooks.com

*Our mission is to publish and distribute inspirational products offering exceptional value and biblical encouragement to the masses.*

Member of the
Evangelical Christian
Publishers Association

Printed in the United States of America.
5 4 3 2 1

# ROOM AT THE INN

# ORANGE BLOSSOM CHRISTMAS

*by Kristy Dykes*

# Chapter 1

The phone rang just as Landon Michael popped a cold capsule in his mouth and washed it down with a glass of juice squeezed from oranges picked from his own grove. He decided to let the voice mail catch the phone call. He felt too wretched to talk to anybody. All he felt like doing was getting back to his recliner and spraying down with a medicated throat spray.

*Ring-g-g-g-g.*

*"Atchoo!"* He reached for a tissue. What if it was someone from the high school? Principals couldn't get sick. At least that's what his staff told him yesterday when he left, coughing up a storm. They said they couldn't do without him, especially with Christmas vacation coming up next week. There was simply too

much work to be done, they told him. Was this his secretary calling? Did she need something important?

*Ring-g-g-g-g.*

He smiled. Was it somebody offering to bring him some homemade chicken soup? But if it was Miss Available-with-a-capital-A home ec teacher Pamela Perkins, well, he'd pass, thank you very much. . . .

*Ring-g-g-g-g, ring-g-g-g-g.*

His sense of duty got the best of him, and he grabbed the phone, determined to squeak out a greeting, raspy though it would be. "Hello?"

"Howdy, there. My name's Pastor Rodney Ellerson callin' from north Georgie. Is this the Orange Blossom Bed and Breakfast Inn?"

Landon coughed.

"I must've dialed the wrong number—"

More coughing.

"Could you tell me if I reached Lake Wallace, Floridy?"

"Yes. Sorry. I've. . .got a. . .terrible head cold."

"What a bad time of year—winter—to get yerself a cold. A cold in cold weather. Why, that's turrible."

Landon looked out the kitchen window and saw the bright-as-summer sun shining down on the clear-as-day lake. He smiled, knowing the thermometer read eighty-eight. "Any time of year is bad to get a cold. *Atchoo.*"

"Yer right about that, pardner. So, this *is* the Orange

Blossom Bed and Breakfast Inn?"

"Yes." What did this caller with the Georgia twang want? Landon glanced out the bank of windows in the great room. Nestled among gigantic orange trees, he saw the little brown wooden house across the road, the Orange Blossom Bed and Breakfast Inn. Nobody had stayed in it since his wife died a year ago. The B and B had been her brainchild. As far as he was concerned, it wasn't a B and B any longer. It was back to its original status—a cracker gothic cottage from Old Florida—what some historians called the early days of Florida. Eons ago, his forebears had built it and lived in it. These days, it was as vacant as a classroom in summer.

"Well," drawled the preacher from north Georgia, "the reason I'm calling is my wife saw an article about the Orange Blossom B and B in her favorite magazine, and she got this idear to book a room for our church secretary as a gift from us and the church. I think it's a right good idear myself. . .I'd even venture to say it's inspired by God, you know, providential, because, you see, our church secretary is the most deservin' person in the whole wide world of a little R & R. . . ."

*Wonder if he's long-winded in the pulpit, too?*

"Why, our church secretary—Lois is her name—just like Lois in the Bible—why, she directs our children's church program, and last Sunday night, she put on the kids' Christmas play with twenty-three wriggly, writhing kids. Ever since she's been our secretary—six months now—our church has grown by leaps and bounds. . .why, she's got as many idears as a doctor's got pills. . .and besides that, she's the most dedicated secretary in church history, I do believe. . . ."

*Bingo. A long-winded talker is a long-winded preacher.* Landon smiled, remembering what his minister-father liked to jokingly say about long-winded visiting preachers. *If they don't strike oil after twenty minutes, they ought to quit boring.*

"And so, we're a-wantin' to book a room. Please say there's room at the inn." He let out a belly laugh. "Get it? Room at the inn? Like in Jerusalem two thousand years ago when Joseph and Mary came a-knockin' on the door of an inn. Please say ya got an empty room at yer B and B. My wife's got her heart set on yer place for Lois. . .it's a little piece of heaven smack dab in the middle of a Florida orange grove, is what she said. Please don't say you're full."

*No, we're not full, that's for certain.* Landon smiled again.

"My wife loved them pictures of the Orange Blossom B and B—that funny-lookin' house a-settin' near a little lake in central Florida, and that was that. There's no other B and B to be had for Lois's R & R, as far as my wife's concerned."

Landon was surprised. The preacher's wife had *just* seen that article? Why, the Orange Blossom B and B had been featured in the magazine over two years ago.

"My wife buys all her magazines at the library for a quarter. 'Course they're a little out of date when she gets them, and sometimes the coupons are ripped out, but that don't bother her none a-tall. We'd like to book a full ten days for Lois"—he paused, and a fumbling noise came across the phone lines—"no, make that eleven days—I just checked my calendar. She'll get there December 15, and she'll leave December 26, the day after Christmas. She'll be arriving next Friday. You take Visa?"

Landon had a coughing fit.

"I knew I hadn't lost ya. I heard ya breathin' the whole time I been a-rattlin' on. Try using nasal spray. Then you won't have to breathe through yer mouth. When ya have to breathe through yer mouth, yer throat gets dried out, ya know? And besides, it sounds turrible. Yep. I knew I hadn't lost ya."

"It. . .hurts. . .to talk."

"I can empy-thize. I had a cold last month. Like I said, I'm real sorry yer sick."

"Thanks."

"My grandpappy always said, 'Take cold medicine, and in seven days you'll be well. Don't take cold medicine, and in seven days you'll be well.' In other words, you'll be as good as new in a week, medicine or not."

"I hope so."

"My credit card number is. . ." The preacher rattled off some numbers.

Landon jotted them down hurriedly.

"Can you send me a brochure?" The preacher rattled off an address. "My name's Pas-tor Rodney Ellerson. Did I say that already? E-l-l-i-s-o-n," he spelled. "Ellerson."

A few minutes later, as Landon plopped in his leather recliner in the great room, he realized with a full-blown case of worry that he now had a guest coming to the long-closed Orange Blossom Bed and Breakfast Inn.

In one week's time!

He glanced out the windows. The cottage across the road needed a thorough cleaning. It was probably covered in dust bunnies and cobwebs. And he was as sick as a dog.

"*Atchoo*." Why had he taken this booking? Maybe it had something to do with the reverend. He liked his down-home flavor. This preacher reminded him of his own father—a minister, too. This preacher had the same quaint Southern drawl and the same penny-pinching-by-necessity ways. His father would be amused when Landon told him about this preacher from north Georgia wanting a room for his secretary.

Maybe it had something to do with what the preacher

said. *My wife's got her heart set on yer place. . .she loved them pictures of your funny-lookin' house a-settin' near a little lake in central Florida.*

Landon sprayed his throat with the vile-tasting green stuff, reflecting on the way the preacher's wife described the Orange Blossom Inn.

A little piece of heaven in a Florida orange grove?

*I may just donate the church secretary's stay. I may not charge the preacher a penny.*

The booking, though, and why he'd done it. . .maybe it had something to do with that poor church secretary. Into his mind popped a picture of his father's church secretary at the church he presently served in North Carolina. . . . Fiftyish. Spinsterish. . .or was it widowish?

Overworked for sure. . . And definitely underpaid.

*This Lois lady with the children's program on her shoulders, as well as a host of other things at her church, will probably enjoy the solitude of the Orange Blossom,* he decided. *She's sure to be refreshed during her stay. It's quiet around here, that's for certain.*

He unwrapped a honey-and-lemon throat lozenge, popped it into his mouth, leaned back, and closed his eyes.

*Somehow I'll manage to get the place cleaned up before she arrives.*

❧

Through a deluge of rain, Lois Delaney drove down the

dark, lonely road in the midst of Florida orange groves, hunting the sign the proprietor said to look for: Orange Blossom Bed and Breakfast Inn.

For long minutes now, she had slowed at every sign, then accelerated past them. Where was that sign? He said to go six miles past the main highway. Hadn't she gone six miles by now? Rats. She should've noted the mileage when she turned off the highway.

Now, she looked carefully at the odometer and decided to go exactly two more miles, then turn back and begin hunting again.

What a time to be arriving at a B and B—and one set in such a remote place. She checked her watch by the light of the dashboard. Five past eleven. But she couldn't help the lateness of the hour. First, she'd gotten a late start. Too many duties in the church office before Christmas. Then, of all things, her windshield wiper motor had broken in south Georgia, and she spent hours in the Toyota dealership while they fixed it. Whoever heard of a windshield wiper motor breaking? And on a new car, at that? If it'd been her old car, she could've understood. She'd driven that thing for nearly seven years, and its windshield wiper motor had *never* given her a problem.

What more could go wrong? Nothing, she assured herself. All would be well shortly. She would soon arrive at the Orange Blossom B and B, fall into a freshly made bed, perhaps a canopied four-poster. And then she would sleep late the next morning, at least past her usual 6:30. Then she would head for the wide front porch for a leisurely and delicious breakfast that included, according to the brochure, freshly squeezed orange juice and orange blossom honey.

At the Orange Blossom B and B, she would meet interesting people from all walks of life. The magazine article showed several guests eating breakfast together on the plank porch. Perhaps she would form lasting friendships with some of the guests. Outgoing and gregarious, she was always making new friends.

During the week, she planned to take walks in the orange grove and around the lake for quiet reflection, something she rarely had time for.

"One thing's for sure," she said aloud as she continued driving at a snail's pace so she could look for the sign through the rain, "I need some quiet reflection. And rejuvenation, too."

She thought about her recent breakup with Phil. Oh, how that had hurt. She was ecstatic when they started a relationship four months ago. After all, the playing field was narrow for a thirty-two-year-old single Christian woman.

Evangelist Phil A. Pullman had held a revival at their church, and from the first, she'd been impressed with—and attracted to—this dashing, debonair minister, charisma dripping off him like the rain now falling from the sky.

But that wasn't why she came to care for him during their four months of e-mails, phone calls, and occasional visits. It was because he truly seemed to care for her. And he was so dedicated to the ministry. And he made her laugh—he was as zany as she was. She recalled the times they belted out hymns together, him singing in his beautiful baritone, her as off-key as the day was long, both of them ending the songs laughing like hyenas.

She remembered the funny name he called himself, a play on words, his eyebrows going up and down every time he said it, her laughing in her usual way, loud and boisterous.

*I'm Evangelist Phil A. Pulpit. Get it? Fill a pulpit. That's what I do.*

Two weeks ago, he wrote her a succinct e-mail that *hadn't* made her laugh. In fact, it made her cry.

*Hi, Lois. I don't know how to say this. This is hard. I enjoyed our times together. I thought we had a future. Two weeks ago, I met Nicole Wilson. She's a preacher's daughter. She sings like an angel, and she even plays the harp! Can you believe that? We've already sung a duet together. "Father, Make Us One" was the song. She's a high soprano, and oh, did we sound good, if I do say so myself. Although she's only eighteen, she'll be a great asset to my ministry. I hope you can understand this. I want you to know, I'll always consider you a friend. Phil*

Lois blinked back a tear, recalling the hurtful E-mail. Just what did her future hold in the man department? "God, are You ever going to send me a man, the right man? If so, when?" Her voice was whiny, but she couldn't help it.

From the time she was a little girl, she'd wanted to be a wife and mother, the best in the world, just like her own mother had been and still was. But so far, life hadn't led her that way. Instead, she became a publicist who was now working as a church secretary temporarily.

"Lord, are You listening?" She wasn't embarrassed about talking to the Lord like this. She and the Lord were on a first-name basis. She had loved the Lord with all her heart, as the scriptures instructed, for her entire life. She and the Lord'd had many conversations.

Now, though, she was doing all the talking. The Lord was mute.

She smiled, remembering a poem she'd recently come across, and she said it now.

*Now I lay me down to sleep,*
*Lord, give me a man for keeps!*

*If there's a man beneath my bed,*
*I hope he heard each word I said!*


She laughed uproariously. "Lord, *please* give me a man, a good Christian man. Think how much we can accomplish for Your kingdom as a team." She paused, contrite. "Okay, Lord. I admit it. That's just a side benefit. The real reason I want a man is because I want someone to care for me, someone I can share my life with, and vice versa."

She slowed for yet another road sign, then proceeded. "Okay, Lord, I'll be quiet so You can speak."

Nothing.

For a couple of minutes, nothing.

"All right, Lord, I've been in this journey of faith long enough to know that when You don't speak I'm supposed to rely on the last word You gave me. And that's this. I'm to continue to draw close to You and believe that You are working things out for my good."

She drove on, the odometer clocking off yet another mile. "There it is," she exclaimed as she made a sharp left turn off the paved road and onto a dirt one. "Orange Blossom B and B, here I come. R & R at the rescue for this heart-weary woman."

She made her way slowly down the dirt road—a quagmire in the rain—as she searched for the B and B.

"Look for a stone-and-stucco home on the left—that's where I live," the proprietor had said. "Then pull into the driveway directly across from it. That's the B and B."

She spotted the stone-and-stucco home—just barely—in the darkness. Her enthusiasm dampened. No lights on the road? The porch? From inside the proprietor's house? The B and B? She wheeled into the driveway of the B and B, just as the proprietor had instructed.

Her headlights flashed on a small wooden structure, the charming wooden cottage pictured in the brochure, and she felt heartened somewhat.

"Orange Blossom B and B," she called out cheerily. "I'm here at last."

She turned off the ignition. Momentarily her automatic headlights went off. What now? It was still drizzling, and besides, no one was about. No people. No cars. No proprietor.

Should she get out and knock on the door? She knew it was 11:30 at night, but she also knew that the proprietor was expecting her. The last time they talked on her cell phone—three hours ago—she told him about her windshield wiper motor mishap. She also told him she would be late. So where was he?

She tooted her horn.

A dog barked at her car window, and her heart leapt to her throat. She looked sideways and saw the biggest dog she'd ever laid eyes on—or so it seemed given the circumstances. He was standing—*standing?*—at her window, his paws on her car door.

"Down, Marmaduke," came a man's gruff voice in the darkness. Then a flashlight came on.

She cranked up the engine and threw the car in reverse.

"Miss Delaney?" The man thumped on her window.

Through the tinted glass she made out a man standing there holding an umbrella, although she couldn't make out his features.

"I thought you weren't coming." He thrust his hand backward, toward the cottage. "This is the Orange Blossom B and B. If you'll get out, I'll show you to your room. And I promise to corral Marmaduke. Don't be afraid of him. He's a great big baby."

Marmaduke let out a howl.

"Hush, Marmaduke." The man petted the dog. "I promise you, his bark is bigger than his bite."

She didn't care to test the man's last statement as the dog let out another ferocious bark. What should she do now? She felt like driving away.

"Miss Delaney?"

She looked straight ahead where her headlights shone, to the little cracker gothic cottage in front of her, saw the wide front porch, noted its charm, and thought about its unique history.

"Your pastor, Reverend Ellison, booked this room for you. I talked with him last week."

Ever the frugal one, she remembered her pastor's hard-earned money that he'd invested in her Christmas vacation.

"It's not luxurious by any means, but I think you'll find it pleasant."

She turned off the ignition. She would at least look things over. "We'll see," she said under her breath.

# Chapter 2

Landon held the umbrella over Miss Delaney as they walked toward the front porch. He'd already tied Marmaduke firmly to a newel post.

He was surprised at Miss Delaney's appearance. When the reverend from north Georgia had said the words "church secretary" on the phone, Landon thought fiftyish and spinsterish—or was it widowish?—simply because of his father's church secretary.

This church secretary was nothing of the sort. Oh, she wasn't a beauty queen, but she was certainly attractive. Her short blond hair had a bounce to it, and he was almost certain her eyes were light blue, a fitting complement, if so. It was too dark to get a good look at them. And her jeans-clad figure was pleasing—not too thin like so many young women. And she seemed friendly, not to mention her mannerliness and politeness.

Once on the porch, he stood the open umbrella at a precise angle to let the raindrops fall down, then shined his flashlight at the door as he unlocked it and pushed it open. "Come on in."

"It's locked?"

"Well. . .yes."

"There aren't any guests staying here? Besides me?"

"Well. . .no."

She didn't say anything.

He felt bad. But he could at least be cheery. "This house is called a cracker gothic cottage."

"I read about it in the brochure. Groovy."

He stepped inside, fumbled for the light switch, and clicked it on. "This is the central hallway. When my ancestors lived here—"

"Your ancestors lived in this house?"

"That's right. Back then, there were no front or back doors to this hall. But we added doors to keep in the AC. The construction is called a—"

"Shotgun?"

"No. A dogtrot. A shotgun is where you can look through the front room and see all the way to the back. In a dogtrot, all the rooms open off of a central hall, kind of like a breezeway. The early settlers were called Florida crackers because many of them had cattle, and when they popped their whips, a *crack* sounded. Anyway, they built their homes this way to catch the breezes."

She clasped her hands to her heart. "Can't you just envision some of your relatives standing right here in this hall?" Enthusiasm dripped off her. "Maybe with a broom in their hands, sweeping? Or the paddle of a churn, making butter? Your great-great-grandmother, perhaps?"

He shrugged. "Never had anybody ask me that. Here's the parlor." He walked into a room on his left, and she followed him in. He made his way to a lamp, turned it on, then another. His wife always said lamplight created a pleasing ambience.

"Welcome to the. . ." He swallowed hard as he glanced around. The place was a mess. Thick dust was everywhere—on the furniture, the whatnots, and the dark-stained pine floors. And a strong musty smell permeated the air. He found his voice. "Welcome to the Orange Blossom Bed and Breakfast Inn."

"Thank you." She wore a shocked expression on her face.

He felt terrible. Miss Available-with-a-capital-A home ec teacher Pamela Perkins had offered to clean up the place for him when she heard about his guest, and he'd gladly taken her up on her offer. He'd been sick with this wretched cold, and the workload at school had been heavy due to the approaching Christmas holidays. For the first time, he'd been glad for Miss Perky Pamela's wily ways. Had she gotten her dates mixed up? For sure. Phooey.

"This is where I'm supposed to get some R & R?" A drop of water hit Miss Delaney on the head, and she gasped, then wiped it off and looked up. A big black mildew stain dotted the tongue-and-groove pine board ceiling.

"The place appears to be a little run-down. . . ."

"I'll say." Another drop of water hit her on the head, and she took two steps forward, away from the steady leak.

"I haven't had the time to devote to the B and B." He looked down at the pine floors, noting the discoloration—apparently from the water dripping from the ceiling. "It's been closed for a year—since my wife passed away. She ran it. I'm a high school principal, and I keep a small herd of cattle, and besides that, I have a ten-acre orange grove. There aren't enough hours in the day to do all that *and* run the B and B." He coughed. All this talking was making his throat act up. Was he getting a relapse? Phooey.

She didn't say a word, but now her expression read "tired."

"Look. I have some explaining to do. I apologize. Big time. A friend was supposed to come clean for me today.

I don't know what happened. But town is eighteen miles down the road. You can follow me, and I'll get you a motel room—at my expense. I'm really embarrassed."

She yawned, stifled it, then extended her hand toward him. "At least let's introduce ourselves first. I'm Lois Delaney. And you? You're Mr. Michael, right?"

"That's right." He reached for her hand, shook it, released it. "Landon Michael."

Sparkles danced in her eyes. "Landon Michael?" she blurted. "As in, Michael Landon?" She laughed uproariously.

Landon didn't know what to think. The woman was standing there laughing at him. Like a hyena? Yes, definitely. If he wasn't a church man and if she wasn't a church secretary, he'd vow she had imbibed.

"Sorry." She looked subdued again, though the sparkles were still in her eyes. "It's just that your name. . ." She laughed—hooted actually. "Landon Michael. . .why, it's the reverse of the late actor's, and you look exactly like him. People ever tell you that?"

"A few."

She hummed the *Bonanza* theme song as her hands strummed an imaginary guitar, a goofy look on her face. "Dum-duh-duh-duh-duh-duh-duh-duh-duh-dum-dah. . . dum-duh-duh-duh-duh-duh-duh-duh-duh-dum-duh-duh-duh-dah." Only she was off-key, way off.

"My grandmother was a fan of *Bonanza* when it was popular. When I was born, she suggested it to my parents." He spoke deadpan-fashion on purpose.

She looked like she was about to cackle again but suddenly regained her composure. "I was only kidding."

He stood there with his arms folded across his chest. He had thought she was mannerly and polite? Ha!

"I'm just being silly—"

*Words well spoken, Miss Zany Delaney.* "So, are you ready to head for town?" His arms were still folded, and he was sure he wore a stern expression. Good. The sooner he got rid of this crazy woman, the better.

"Look." She took a step toward him. "I have some explaining to do. I apologize. Big time."

He had said those very words earlier. In that exact order. He was somewhat amused. And curious about her.

"I'm really embarrassed."

He dropped his arms. *There she goes again. Repeating me.* He smiled.

"I didn't mean to be so silly. I've been told I'm zany. . . ."

*Bingo.*

"But I've also been told I'm smart. And it wasn't too smart of me to laugh about your name. It's just that I'm so tired. . . ." She let out a long sigh. "And I had such a bad day, what with the late start, and then the rain, and then my windshield wiper motor breaking—whoever heard of a windshield wiper motor breaking, and on a new car, at that? And then the long delay to get it fixed, and then more rain, and then I couldn't find your place, and it got later and later, and finally I arrived and found this"—she gestured all around her—"a defunct bed and breakfast, and I. . .I—"

"I understand." He threw up his hand, traffic cop style, chuckling. "Tell you what. If you'll forgive me for this," he said, pointing to the room, "I'll forgive you for laughing at my name. Agreed?" He thrust out his palm. "Let's shake on it, okay?"

"Okay." She held out her hand.

The moment he touched her, something happened to him. He couldn't hang words on it, so he tucked it inside to contemplate later. "Come on. Let's get this place locked up, and then we'll be on our way."

"I've decided to stay."

"You have?"

"Y—yes, I. . .I have."

He heard the catch in her voice. Was something going on with her, too? He looked long and hard at her. "If you're sure, then?"

"I'm s—sure."

❦

In her plaid shorty pajamas, Lois put the sheets on the

iron bedstead in the charming little room, looking forward to crawling into bed after such a long day. Why had she suddenly decided to stay? Especially after Mr. Michael offered to get her a motel room in town? She wasn't sure.

When she told him her decision, he had shown her about the place, opening and closing the doors of the bedrooms, the kitchen, the large pantry, and the two bathrooms.

"These aren't original to the house, of course," he'd told her. "People used privies out back in the old days."

Then he insisted on bringing in her luggage in the drizzle without her help. She was a little embarrassed. She tended to pack things in small bags, and some of them had items spilling out of them, like her hair dryer and curling iron and other stuff. But he managed to get her things in without dropping anything in the wet grass.

Then he vaulted across the dirt road to his house and returned with bedding—sheets, pillows, towels, and even a new-looking comforter.

"The bed's made," he'd told her when he got back, "but it's been a whole a year. Needs changing. Even the comforter."

He offered to help her make it, but she said she would do it herself.

"Be sure to open some windows," he said. "This place

needs airing out. Tomorrow I'll see about getting it cleaned." Then he apologized again for the inconvenience and left.

"Inconvenience?" She pulled the comforter over the sheets, thinking about the leaky ceiling and stained floors in the parlor. "It doesn't matter about the inconvenience, Mr. Michael Landon, I mean, Landon Michael. What matters is that you're letting a piece of living history disintegrate right before your eyes."

She dug in one of her bags for her facial cleanser, then trudged to the bathroom. "How unique, to own a cracker gothic cottage. Don't you realize how valuable this place is? Maybe not in monetary terms, but certainly in the historic sense."

She washed her face and dried it on a towel he'd brought over. "Haven't you ever heard the saying 'A stitch in time saves nine'? The longer you let this cottage go, the more it'll cost you to bring it back up to par. Oh, well. It's none of my business. What *is* my business is to get some rest."

She walked to the window, raised the shade a few inches, and opened the window just as high. A pitter-patter of rain greeted her, an inviting sound to her now. Across the room, she raised the other window the same few inches.

"The raindrops'll sing me to sleep." She smiled as she

pulled down the bedding and crawled in.

As her head hit the pillow, her mind turned to the question that had been gnawing at her. Why did she decide to stay? After her disappointment of seeing the place dirty and in disrepair? Not to mention the lack of interesting guests?

She yawned. She was sure she'd stayed because of her fatigue. Yes, that was it, wasn't it? Tomorrow she would probably leave. This was no place for a vacation.

Like a vapor, the face of Michael Landon—correction, Landon Michael—appeared before her eyes. Was she dreaming? She didn't think so. She saw him with that charming grin, then with that stern expression which only intrigued her more.

She thought about his comical name. What was his mother thinking when she named him? She recalled his handsome good looks, just like the late actor's. Dark bushy hair. Sun-burnished skin. Taut, well-formed muscles. She thought about his interesting life. High school principal. Cattleman. Grove owner.

She thought about the spark that passed between them when they shook hands that second time. For some reason, across her mind now flitted the face of Phil. Then Landon. Then Phil. Then Landon. Then Phil. Then Landon. She was so tired. Was her mind playing tricks on her?

"The Orange Blossom B and B." She was as wide awake as all get-out. "An R & R retreat? Looks like S & W to me—stress and worry."

# Chapter 3

Lois awoke the next morning in the strange surroundings with a start. What time was it? She
glanced at her wristwatch. Nine thirty-five! She
hadn't slept this late for eons, even on Saturdays like it
was today.

She breathed in deeply. Was she smelling some kind
of air freshener? She recalled the proprietor's promise.
*Tomorrow I'll see about getting this place cleaned.*

She sat up in bed, refreshed in her spirit. Had a cleaning lady already been here—in this very room as she
slept—swishing fragrant spray around? Had the cleaning
lady used flower-scented furniture polish, perhaps? But a
quick glance at the dusty bedside table told her that no
cleaning lady had been on these premises today.

A movement at the window caught her eye, and she

looked that way. The curtains were swaying in a gentle morning breeze. She pushed back the covers, jumped up, and was across the room in a flash. She raised the shade all the way up and was met with a dose of sunshine that warmed her soul. She raised the window as far as it would go and saw a sight to behold.

Orange trees thick with orange blossoms—and as fragrant as the perfume counter at the mall.

"Well, what do you know. So that's what I'm smelling." She couldn't get over it. Everywhere she looked, she saw orange trees dotted with fragrant white flowers. She was itching to get outside and explore the surroundings.

She ran to the other side of the room, threw up the shade, then the window. She saw a shimmering lake, as clear as crystal. Tied to a dock was a dinghy. To her far left, across the dirt road, she saw Mr. Michael's sprawling stucco home. Beyond that was a barn and a few head of cattle grazing in a field. She even heard a distinctive moo in the distance. She was touched by the idyllic scene, her heart encouraged.

Sure, there were no interesting guests here. Sure, the place needed a deep cleaning and some repairs. But the orange groves. . .and the lake. . .and the charm of the cracker gothic cottage and its grounds. . .they wooed her like a beau to a girl.

She heard the front door open. *Click.* She heard it close. *Click.*

She froze in her steps. Who was in the house? Mr. Landon—correction, Mr. Michael?

"Oops," she whispered. "I've got to get his name right." Was Mr. Michael in the wide front hall? As far as she knew, he was the only one on the premises. She looked down at her shorty pajamas. She dashed to her suitcase and rummaged for her robe, but couldn't find it.

She remembered throwing it in a small satchel at the last minute. She scrounged the satchel's contents, found her robe, and threw it on, her stomach growling fiercely. She walked back to the door.

"Mr. Michael?" she said through the door. No answer. She cracked the door a peep and called his name again, with the same result. She opened the door six inches and stuck her head out. "Mr. Michael?" Still no answer. But a new scent assailed her. Food.

She saw an open door at the end of the wide hallway—the kitchen she remembered from last night's brief tour. She left her room, walked to the kitchen, and on the table, she saw a luscious sight. Breakfast—and a note propped up.

*Please enjoy your breakfast. And make yourself*
*at home. When you're ready to venture out, come*

*look me up. I'm across the road doing paperwork.*
*The cleaning lady is on standby. While she's here,*
*I'd like to show you around the place, if that's okay*
*with you.*

*Landon*

"Yum, yum." She sat down at the table and partook. Sausage-in-biscuits, flaky and hot. Orange blossom honey and various jams. Chunks of fresh fruit. Orange juice. A choice of hot tea or coffee in tiny carafes.

All were pleasingly arranged on a large silver tray. She noted that the cloth napkins matched the dishes, both dotted with tiny white flowers in the midst of green leaves. Orange blossoms? Amazing. The crystal vase in the middle of the tray held. . .an orange blossom bouquet? Wonderful. She leaned forward and buried her nose in the flowers, drawing in a deep lungful of fragrance. She hadn't felt this carefree in a long time.

She stood up and did a joy jig, let out a victory yell, though a subdued "Yee-haw!" then sat back down and took a sip of her hot tea.

"As I said last night, Orange Blossom B and B"—she glanced around the room—"I'm here at last."

She smiled, a chant-poem forming in her mind, and she said it aloud.

*I'm here at last*
*I'm here to stay.*
*I'm ready for adventures*
*To come my way!*

With Miss Delaney's breakfast delivered, Landon came out of the cottage, made his way down the front steps, and headed toward the backyard. He needed to get some logs from the wood stack. Moments later, his arms laden, he walked down the side of the cottage on his way to his house across the road.

"Yee-haw," came Miss Delaney's voice from somewhere inside the cottage.

He rolled his eyes then chuckled. "Miss Zany Delaney, you're at it again." He crossed the dirt road, went inside his house, and deposited the logs on the hearth. Would they get some chilly weather in time for Christmas so he could light a fire?

He smiled, thinking about his usual procedure during Florida winters—a brightly burning fire in the hearth with the AC cranked up on high. That was about the only way Floridians could enjoy a fire, at least the ones in central and south Florida.

He crossed the hardwood floors of the great room and entered the French doors that led into his book-lined study. As he said in his note to Miss Delaney, he intended to do some paperwork this morning.

He sat down at his desk and in moments was engrossed.

*Knock-knock.*

He heard the brass knocker on the front door, looked up from his work, glanced at the clock. More than an hour had passed since he'd sat down. He strode out of the study and made his way to the door. He swung it open and saw Miss Delaney standing there.

"Mr. Michael, your note said to come find you." She was on the sidewalk leading up to the covered front entry. Apparently, she'd knocked on the door, then stepped back out in the sunshine.

Landon stood in the open doorway, his hand on the knob. The sun caught her blond hair at just the right angle, and it looked like the proverbial spun gold. She made a movement and her hair bounced just as it had last night. Indeed, her eyes were light blue. Azure? Yes. She was in jeans again, but this time she wore a red knit top that played up the vivid color in her complexion. Another proverbial saying came to mind: peaches and cream.

"Mr. Michael?" She was cupping her eyebrows against the sun.

"Uh, yes. Come in, Miss Delaney."

"It's Lois."

"And call me Landon, please."

"Sure, Landon." She stepped inside then paused and looked around. "Thank you for the delicious breakfast. I appreciate it."

"You're welcome." He stood there with his hand still on the knob. As she passed him, her scent smelled better than the orange blossoms outside or the Christmas tree inside. His sense of smell had finally returned after his dreadful cold, and he breathed her scent in deeply. Was it her shampoo? Her cologne? Those body sprays women used?

"What a beautiful home you have." Her gaze roamed the room.

"Thanks." His gaze followed hers. Gleaming hardwood floors. Elegant though comfortable furniture. Soaring ceilings. Oversized windows that framed the magnificent outdoors. The adjacent kitchen with its long inviting bar and stools, a big French country table beyond.

"Did your wife do the decorating or you?"

"She did. That's not my forte."

"She was talented, I'll say." She let out a low whistle. "This looks like something from those decorating shows on TV. The only shows I like are the ones that feature remodels of old houses. Just like you, decorating's not my forte, either. Ever watch those shows?"

He shrugged and shook his head. His TV stayed tuned to sports and the political commentary shows. And the news, of course.

"That's about all the TV I watch. I recently saw one on Willa Cather's refurbished Nebraska family home. Groovy, huh?"

He was amused by her use of the word "groovy." That was as passé as tie-dye. The teenagers that attended his high school certainly didn't say *groovy*.

"Oh, and I love old-timey movies. And reruns, too. I can't stand those shows where all they do is argue about politics. I don't watch too much of the news, either. It's so depressing. And I hate all those incessant sports programs. When I was growing up, when my father wasn't doing remodeling jobs, he ate, drank, and slept sports. I guess that's why I can't stand them now."

He smiled a wry smile.

"Would you like me to sit down?" She sank down on one of the two leather sofas flanking the fireplace and looked over at him, sparkles dancing in her eyes again, like she was baiting him.

He shut the door and came toward her. "Of course." *I would've asked if you'd given me the chance.* He rubbed his temples. "Sorry. It's just that I've been so absorbed this morning." He sat down in his recliner.

She leaned forward, her brows arched. "You said you'd show me about?"

"Yes."

"The Orange Blossom B and B is just like my pastor's

wife described. A little piece of heaven. Of course she's more than my pastor's wife. She's my aunt. And my pastor is my uncle—"

"Reverend Ellison?"

She nodded. "I was working in Atlanta. I'm a publicist. When my firm downsized, Uncle Rodney and Aunt Clovis begged me to come work with them in their church in Milton, Georgia, for a little while before I took another position."

Absently, she toyed with her hair. "I'm not sure why I took them up on it. Big-city girl versus small-town ingénue." She let out a gentle laugh.

Landon settled back in his recliner. Was she as long-winded as Reverend Ellison?

"The town, Milton, is quaint, and so are the church and the people. Quaint means 'pleasingly old-fashioned.' Never thought I'd like that lifestyle, but I do. In fact, I love Milton." She laughed her bright hyena-like laughter. "I've always had a love for antiques and historical things. I guess that's why I like living there so much."

*Bingo. I was right. You're as long-winded as good old Uncle Rodney.*

"Ever visit Atlanta?" Again, she didn't wait for a response. "There's a restaurant named after a character out of *Gone With the Wind*." She clasped her hands together. "I love that story. I've visited the Margaret Mitchell house several times. It's where she actually wrote *Gone With the Wind*. And I've read two biographies of her. What's that title I just finished?" Her brows drew together, and she tapped on her chin.

*You are one dramatic lady,* he thought as she rattled on.

"Can't say I like everything about Scarlett O'Hara. Basically, she was a self-centered girl who lacked a sense of humor. But there's one thing I *do* like about her. She always had an optimistic bent. I'd like to think that I have that quality, too. Remember what she said when Rhett left her?" She fluttered her eyelashes, then threw her hand across her heart. " 'I'll think about it tomorrow. After all, tomorrow is another day.' " She gave Landon a saucy smile. "Don't you love positive, upbeat people? But I've gone on and on. I tend to do that when I'm real excited."

Landon stared at her. *This woman could talk the hind legs off a billy goat. Why, she zips from one subject to the next. I've never seen anything like it. She started out with her aunt and uncle and ends up impersonating Scarlett O'Hara. Talk about drama?*

"In my little town—"

*Ring-g-g-g-g. . .*

Landon looked heavenward. *Thank You, Jesus.* He edged forward. *I'm saved by the bell.*

*Ring-g-g-g-g. . .*

"Excuse me while I get the phone." *Miss Zany Delaney.*

"Sure. Take your time."

He made his way into the study. It was probably his cleaning lady calling. Early this morning he'd gotten ahold of her, and it just so happened that she had a cancellation today. That worked perfectly for him. Forget Miss Perky Pamela. He should've booked his cleaning lady from the beginning, but Pamela'd been so insistent about helping him.

A minute or two later, he emerged from his study and walked toward Lois. "Are you ready for your tour? That was the cleaning lady. She's on her way over."

"Ready." Lois rose to her feet.

*Knock-knock.*

"Wonder who that is?" Landon headed for the front door, puzzled. "The cleaning lady couldn't've gotten here that quick, and we don't have solicitors this far out." He threw open the door. There stood Pamela.

"Hi, Landon."

He tried not to stare. Tall, dark-haired, and tanned, with model-perfect features, Pamela was dressed in gym shorts that showed off her shapely legs and a tiny tank top that revealed—oh, never mind. He couldn't help noticing that her shorts hung below her waist and her top ended just above. A gentleman, he looked beyond her to the orange grove across the way. What did women think these days? Didn't they have any idea what their clothing did to a man? Or, rather, lack of clothing? And Pamela was a Christian, to boot!

"I came to clean the cottage like I promised." Pamela put her foot on the planter beside the door, leaned over, and tied her shoe, looking up at him the whole time. "May I have the key?"

Landon squirmed at the distressing view Pamela was displaying. What cottage? What key? Was her tank top getting tinier? Or was her skin growing in circumference? Bingo on both. Where was a man supposed to look? He focused on the grove again. *Keep me true, Lord Jesus, keep me true,* he silently sang—no, belted out—inside. *Keep me true, Lord Jesus, keep me true. . . .*

"Earth to Landon, as we're always saying at school. Are you reading me? I'm reading you loud and clear, Landon, and you're in la-la land. Par for the course." Pamela smiled brilliantly, which only made her beauty more striking.

He finally found his voice. "Come in, Pamela." He gestured inside. "I'd like you to meet someone." For some reason, he couldn't remember his guest's name. Lois Lane?

Lois was at his side in a flash. She thrust out her hand as Pamela took a step into the great room. "Hi, I'm Lois Delaney, and I'm a guest at the Orange Blossom. It's a pleasure to meet you. Pamela, isn't it?"

Landon waited in the yard for Lois to come out of the cottage. She'd run inside to get something after Pamela left. He was going to show Lois around his acreage, take her to the groves, the lake, and the barn as he promised.

*You'd think they were long-lost friends, those two, the way they carried on when I introduced them.*

Lois had a sanguine personality, for sure. Just knowing her for one day, he was fairly certain she never met a stranger.

He guessed that was a good thing—to be so outgoing. She must have tons of friends because she certainly showed herself friendly.

And she was definitely optimistic, something she referred to when she talked about Scarlett O'Hara. He had to admit her cheerfulness—loud though it was at times—was. . .was. . .endearing.

Endearing? He'd have to think about that, but it had a nice ring.

# Chapter 4

Lois sat in Landon's church the next day, though not on the same pew, of course. Yesterday afternoon, when he'd finished showing her around his place, he mentioned that she could follow him to church on Sunday if she wanted to. She decided to take him up on it. Then she called Pamela and asked if she could sit with her. Now, in church, Pamela sat at her side. It was nice having a new friend.

Lois looked down at her hands, saw the rosy glow coming from the stained glass windows, glanced up at the beamed ceiling, and admired the beauty of the sanctuary. She liked the style of this church service. Though it wasn't as countrified as Uncle Rodney's church in north Georgia, it had a pleasant, homey feel. The friendliness of the people, the mixture of choruses and hymns, and the emphasis on children—as evidenced by a musical number by a kids' choir—all appealed to her.

Late yesterday afternoon, after she had freshened up following Landon's tour of his acreage, she headed for the café in town for supper, the one he'd told her about.

Funny. He was there, too, eating. He was almost finished with his meal when she arrived, but he asked her to join him. Out of obligation? After all, she was a paying guest in his B and B, and he'd spent half the day trying to make his guest feel at home. Out of courtesy? He was certainly a gentleman, she knew, though she'd only known him a short while.

"Please stand for the reading of God's Word," the minister said from the oak pulpit. "Brothers and sisters, turn to Psalm thirty-seven, verses four through six."

Lois and Pamela stood, their Bibles in hand, the pages turned to the verses.

" 'Delight yourself in the Lord and he will give you the desires of your heart,' " the minister read. " 'Commit your way to the Lord; trust in him and he will do this: He will make your righteousness shine like the dawn, the justice of your cause like the noonday sun.' " Then he prayed. "You may be seated."

The congregation took their seats.

Lois couldn't help noticing a little old lady on the front pew still standing, even after everyone sat down.

"That's Sister Gladys." Pamela leaned in close with her whispered comment. "She's a dear. Someone faithfully picks her up from the nursing home every Sunday. Sadly, she's suffering from senile dementia." She pointed to her temple, a compassionate look on her face.

Lois nodded in understanding. In their church in north Georgia, it was Miss Mavene. Similar lady. Similar circumstances. So sad.

Lois focused on Sister Gladys's clothing. Similar attire to Miss Mavene's. Sister Gladys was wearing a stained yellow pantsuit and green and white tennis shoes. Perched precariously atop her head was a black velvet pillbox hat, and on her arm hung a white oversized purse that bore jagged lines of blue ballpoint ink.

"Dear ones," the minister intoned, "today we are going to look at three short scriptures. But they pack a powerful punch. The key words are delight, commit, and trust."

Sister Gladys leaned down and picked up a magazine from her pew, then stood upright and held the magazine out at arm's length. She bent yet again, pulled a saucer-sized magnifying glass out of her purse, and peered through it, studying the magazine.

Lois couldn't help smiling. Sister Gladys was holding a tabloid paper. Only it was upside down.

"If we delight in the Lord," the minister said, "the

Bible says He will give us the desires of our hearts. It goes on to say that if we commit our way to Him and trust in Him, He will make our righteousness shine like the dawn and the justice of our cause like the noonday sun. What does all of that mean for us?"

He adjusted the gooseneck of his microphone on the pulpit. "It means, among other things, that the Lord will answer our prayers, vindicate us, and give us guidance."

Sister Gladys shouted "Amen, Brother Ben!" and muttered something nonsensical as she sat down with a thud.

Lois heard tittering among the crowd, saw people squelching chuckles, and smothered her own. Poor Sister Gladys. Miss Mavene in north Georgia never hollered out in a church service, though her oddities included walking around the altar during Uncle Rodney's sermons—until Uncle Rodney appointed one of the women to sit by her. He would never bar the door of the church to people like that. They needed Christian love and compassion even more, was his reasoning, and Lois's, too.

Lois glanced across the aisle and spotted Landon. *Wonder what he is thinking about Miss Gladys's antics?* Yesterday she'd detected that he had a slight sense of humor, but it was so. . .so. . .wry. Then another question loomed in her mind. Why was she even thinking about what Landon was thinking?

*It's only natural,* she told herself. *He's a Christian, he's unattached, and he's good-looking.* She squelched a chuckle that threatened to gurgle up her throat and reveal her thoughts. . .

*I'm saved. . .*

*I'm single. . .*

*And I'm searching!*

*Psalm 37? Where are you?* She bowed her head. *Lord, forgive me for letting my mind wander. But sometimes a girl just can't help herself!*

❦

Late that afternoon on the way home, Landon couldn't quit thinking about Lois. At the close of the church service, the pastor's wife had walked to the platform and invited all singles to the pastor's home for Sunday dinner.

For over two hours, the dozen or so singles—from college-aged to senior citizens—all of them women except him—had enjoyed good fellowship. After the lunch of delicious meat loaf and scalloped potatoes and all the trimmings, they went outside to the backyard and sat in lawn furniture in the pleasant December sunshine.

Landon had spent that time with the pastor, talking sports and politics. The women had chattered like magpies, Lois at the center of the bunch, making them laugh with her stories and antics. He could clearly see and hear her the entire time he chatted with the pastor.

He remembered more of her antics, when they were

leaving and she was on her way down the front steps of the pastor's home and dropped her purse, its contents tumbling to the ground. She had laughed in her crazy way. He had never seen such an array of stuff in all his life. She had everything but the kitchen sink. Talk about a pack rat. Talk about disorganized.

Driving along now, he retrieved a napkin from the glove compartment, cleaned a spot on the windshield, swiped the dashboard, then dropped it into the little waste bag hanging from the radio knob. Into his mind popped a ditty from his childhood.

*He likes me. He likes me not. He likes me. He likes me not.*

He remembered how the girls would pull petals off buttercups as they chanted those two lines. Whichever line they ended up with on the last petal was supposed to be the truth of the matter. Only, in his mind the chant came out a different way.

*I like her. I like her not. I like her. I like her not.*

Yes, he liked Lois's dedication to the Lord. No, he didn't like her loud boisterousness. Yes, he liked her kindness, especially to people like Sister Gladys. At the close of the service this morning, he had seen her chatting with the elderly lady, then hugging her.

"Phooey," he said aloud as he turned onto his dirt road. "I don't have to like or dislike Lois Delaney. She's only a guest at the Orange Blossom. In a week, she'll be history."

Somehow, that thought didn't bring him comfort.

❦

Lois spent Sunday evening in quiet reflection, what she promised herself she would do at the Orange Blossom, though it was totally out of character for her. Give her people to surround her. Give her fun times. That was what refreshed her. But she determined to keep her promise to herself.

All evening, she read a little—from the stack of books she brought along. She also thought a little. But mostly, she rested. Around eight o'clock, she went to the fridge and took out the meat loaf sandwich and iced tea the pastor's wife had insisted she bring home.

She sat down on the divan in the parlor of the quaint cracker gothic cottage, enjoying the delicious supper. Her eye caught and held the big black mildew spot on the ceiling. It had leaked so long, there was a hole that needed patching.

Tomorrow morning she would go into town and buy some lunch meat for a picnic down by the lake. She might even find a hardware store and see if they sold tongue-and-groove pine for the ceiling repair. If they did, she could tell Landon about it. Maybe she could help him fix it. Of course, that would necessitate a roof repair. You couldn't fix a damaged ceiling without addressing the problem behind it. But that was okay. With her expertise, she could help him fix the roof, too.

"Thank you, Uncle Rodney and Aunt Clovis, for this wonderful vacation." She put her feet on the ottoman in front of her. "It's just what I needed."

# Chapter 5

Bright and early, Lois was up, and she found breakfast on the kitchen table as usual. This morning she noticed it was crisply fried bacon, buttery croissants, and watermelon wedges. And of course the orange blossom honey, orange juice, and hot tea.

She crossed to the kitchen windows, opened them, breathed in the luscious scent of orange blossoms, walked back to the table, and sat down. "I'll never forget that smell. It's heaven on earth."

She drew in another lungful of orange blossoms. "Maybe someone sells an orange blossom body spray. I'll have to check out the mall in Atlanta on my way home." Another wave of the tantalizing scent wafted into the room borne on a morning breeze. "That would be fabulous, to smell like orange blossoms all year 'round."

She put a dollop of honey on her croissant, then bowed her head. "Lord, I thank You for this day. I thank You for Your goodness. Oh, Father, You are such a good God. You saved me, You kept me, and You take such loving care of me, all the time. You said You would supply my needs, and You have. You said You would be a friend who sticks closer than a brother, and You are. You said You would never leave me nor forsake me, and You haven't."

She paused, thinking about her recent heartache with Phil. The Lord had been there with her, had seen her through. She jumped to her feet, did a little joy jig. "Yee-haw." She sat back down. *Thank You, Father, thank You, thank You, thank You. Help me to praise You always. In Jesus' name, I pray. Amen.*

*You are delighting in Me, daughter,* the Lord seemed to whisper.

She kept her eyes closed, enjoying the feeling of one-ness with the Lord. She remembered the minister's sermon yesterday. She'd read Psalm 37:4–6 many times. But today, just now, it became real to her as she meditated on the tender voice of the Lord she was hearing.

"Lord," she prayed, "I truly want to be used for Your kingdom and Your glory. . . ."

*That's more delighting. . . .*

"Let my life count for You. . . ."

*I am delighted that you are delighting in Me.*

She opened her eyes, feeling spiritually refreshed, feeling better than last evening when she'd felt physically refreshed. She looked down, saw the honey in one hand and the croissant in the other hand. They were both speaking to her.

*Eat me.*

She smiled as she snapped her eyes shut. "P.S., Lord. Thank You for this food which I am about to eat. Bless the hands that prepared it."

She laughed out loud, a vision of Landon appearing before her eyes. . . . He was wearing a big white chef's apron as he fried bacon in his spacious granite-and-cherry kitchen.

"Oops. Forgive me, Lord, for my wandering mind. I really do thank You for this food. Bless it to the nourishment of my body. In Jesus' name, I pray. Amen."

She took a bite of the delicious honey-dotted croissant—surely heavenly ambrosia. She chewed slowly, thinking about Landon again. Only this time, he wasn't frying bacon. . . .

He was holding her close. . . .

She dropped her utensil, a glob of gooey honey puddling by her plate, but she didn't wipe it up. Instead, she sat there absently running her finger around the rim of her teacup.

The vision appeared again. . . . She and Landon were standing in the orange grove beneath the blossoms, his arms around her, her head on his shoulder. . . .

Then the vision faded. She didn't know what to think, what to say. So she said what popped in her mind.

"Amen, Brother Ben!"

⁂

Landon glanced up from his supper in the town café and saw Lois stepping through the doorway. He stood, gesturing at the empty chair across from him. "Hi, Lois. Won't you have a seat?"

She hesitated, her cheeks pinker than usual.

Hmm. Why was she hesitating? Was she blushing? If he didn't know better, he'd say she was acting shy. And that wasn't the way of Miss Zany Delaney. But he liked it, this uncharacteristic shyness.

Absently, she fiddled with the clasp on her purse.

He wondered. Why was she acting so awkward? "Won't you join me?" He gestured at the empty chair for the second time.

"I wouldn't want to interrupt you again. You were so kind to invite me to sit with you Saturday night. There are plenty of tables in here." She looked about.

He took a step forward, napkin in hand. "No, really. I'd like for you to sit with me."

She smiled at last, walked to his table, and situated

herself in the chair as he tucked it in from behind her.

"Alberta's serving fried chicken and peach cobbler tonight." He sat down opposite her, gesturing at his heaping plate.

"Alberta?"

"The cook. Every Monday night, it's fried chicken."

"Yum, yum. Sounds good to me."

The waitress appeared, took her order, and sauntered off.

"So, what did you do last night and all day today?" He took a swallow of iced tea, set it down, then pushed his plate back an inch or so.

"Please. Go ahead and eat. Yours'll be cold if you wait on mine."

"That's okay."

"No, it's not. I told you I didn't want to discombobulate you, as my great-grandmother would've said."

"Discombobulate?"

She giggled. "Upset. Confuse. Please. Go ahead and eat."

He smiled, picked up his fork and knife, and cut into his chicken. "So, how have you whiled away your time at the Orange Blossom B and B thus far?" He took a bite.

"I'm relaxed, refreshed, and recharged. That says it all."

"Sounds like advertising copy." He threw her a wry smile.

She laughed, her eyes dancing. "I've used my thesaurus a million times in my publicist work. Like you said, at times, colorful descriptions are advertising copy and nothing else. But relaxed, refreshed, and recharged is really true about the Orange Blossom B and B. I could even add revitalized."

"How about refueled?"

"Definitely."

"Let's do some more synonymizing."

"Synonymizing?" She wiggled her eyebrows, looking mischievous.

He fixed his eyes on her, intrigued. "Yes, synonymizing." He was baiting her, what she'd done to him in his great room. He was enjoying this interchange with her, and he wanted to prolong it.

"Hmm." She smiled. "So, you want more synonyms. Let's see. . ."

The waitress set a plate in front of her, then a glass of iced tea.

Lois picked up her fork. "You already pray?"

He nodded. "But I'll do it again." He closed his eyes. "Lord, bless Lois's food. And bless her. In Jesus' name. Amen."

She took a bite of mashed potatoes swimming in gravy.

He didn't know why he'd added "And bless her." It

just came out. "Getting back to our synonymizing, how about regenerated?"

She nodded and dabbed at her lips with her napkin. "Renewed."

"How about rejuvenated?"

"Well said. That's what happens in this little piece of heaven. Rejuvenation."

He chuckled. "I like that description of the Orange Blossom. A little piece of heaven. Your pastor's wife said that."

She nodded. "Aunt Clovis. That's where I got it from. And just think. She hasn't even been here. She's only seen those pictures in the magazine and the brochure. They don't do justice to this place."

He finished eating and put his napkin on the table. "How about rapturous?"

She nodded.

"Transported."

Her eyes sparkled. "To heaven."

They both laughed.

"Heaven?" He drummed his fingers on the table. "Eden."

"New Jerusalem."

"Celestial bliss."

"Celestial bliss? You're good." Her eyes were fairly dancing. "Let's see. The inheritance of the saints in light."

"Wow, you're good, too. Holy City."

"Island of the blessed."

"Happy hunting ground."

"Happy hunting ground?" Her eyebrows arched. Then they drew together, like she was contemplating something. "Hunting, did you say?"

He nodded. "Are you hunting something?"

"You could say that." She threw him one of his own wry grins and a shrug of her shoulders.

"Well, you know what they say." He leaned toward her.

"What?"

"The wish is the father to the thought."

# Chapter 6

For several days, Landon's path seemed to cross with Lois's constantly, though it was entirely unplanned. He couldn't help comparing her with Miss Perky Pamela. Pamela was blatant in her manner. Lois was unpretentious. Pamela was a schemer, it seemed. Lois was more *que sera sera*. Whatever will be, will be.

Pamela dressed like a fashion model and complained about getting dirty. Lois dressed casually, though she was as pretty as a fresh-peeled carrot, as his grandfather would've said about her. She was always in jeans, except for last Sunday's church service. And she never complained about getting dirty. In fact, Monday evening at the town café, she'd asked if she could help him repair the roof and ceiling of the cottage.

On Tuesday morning, they'd tackled the job. Though

he wasn't adept at that type of work, under her expert guidance—she said she'd learned under her father's tute-lage—Landon found that the task wasn't too difficult. Maybe he would take her advice and keep the cottage running as a B and B. At the least, he decided he would keep it clean and in good repair.

Each evening—Tuesday, Wednesday, and Thursday—he had asked her to ride into town with him to eat at the café.

"It's only reasonable," he'd said. "No need for two cars to be going to the same place."

"And no need to waste the gas," she'd added, after accepting his invitations.

That didn't matter to him. That wasn't the reason why he invited her to ride in his car. He couldn't really say what the reason was, exactly, except that he liked her company.

One morning, she asked him about the newborn calf he'd mentioned, and he took her to see it in his motor-ized horse—his pickup truck. She'd peppered him with questions about his orange grove, and they had a picnic there, him explaining the orange-growing process, which she said was fascinating.

She inquired about the high school where he worked, and he took her on a tour of the empty building, since the students were on Christmas break. He told her about the calling he felt from God to work with young people in the role of principal.

"As a high school principal, I feel like I'm a missionary to students," he told her.

"How wonderful," she'd responded, admiration clearly in her eyes.

She'd asked him about the dinghy tied to his dock, and he took her out in it several times. Once, they wore swimsuits and he took her to the sandy beach on the far bank where he'd swum as a child when his grandparents owned the property. They took a refreshing swim that day, and she said she couldn't get over swimming at Christmastime. He told her that he learned to ski on this very lake on a Christmas Day. He was just past toddlerhood, he said. His grandfather had patiently taught him even though it took about a dozen attempts. Every time after that, though, he stood up immediately on those tiny skis, flying across the lake. He told her he was looking for another ski boat right now. His last one he'd recently sold, he said.

During those several days, she told him a lot about herself, about her work in public relations, and about the awards she'd won in the field, all to the glory of God, she said. When she talked about her desire to put the Lord first in her life, he found himself marveling.

In turn, she told him how much she admired him for

his dedication as a high school principal. It was like they had a mutual admiration society going, but he felt they were both sincere in their kind comments to each other.

Enter Miss Pamela Perkins. Somehow, she'd managed to get in on some of his and Lois's times together. The three of them ate together one evening at the café, and the day he showed Lois the high school where he worked, they bumped into Pamela. She was coming out of her home ec classroom carrying boxes of Christmas ornaments.

"I'm going to put these on my tree at home." She tipped her head at the boxes. "I'm putting the finishing touches on it today. I chose a real tree this year instead of an artificial one. Why don't you two join me for Christmas Eve dinner so you can see my tree, and I'll cook us something good to eat?"

So, plans were made for Christmas Eve at Pamela's.

"Pamela *is* a good cook," he told Lois later. "Beats the town café. And that's saying a lot, because Alberta's cooking is the best—as you can attest." He laughed when he rhymed the words.

She laughed, too, at his little rhyme. "I wish I could cook a decent meal. Cooking's not my strong suit."

"But you've got other strong suits." He was thinking of her expertise on the roof and in the field of public relations. He also thought about her devotion to God and church work. He didn't believe he had ever run across a young woman like her, one who seemed to. . .to. . .commune with God. That was a good way of putting it.

Being a minister's son, he liked that quality most of all.

# Chapter 7

Fresh from the shower, with her plaid robe on, Lois stood in front of the pine dresser in her room and blow-dried her hair, then put on her usual light application of makeup. Mascara, blush, and lipstick.

Today, Saturday, she was going to a Christmas party at a church member's house. Tonight, back at the B and B, it would be time for quiet reflection again, something she was looking forward to. Tomorrow morning was a Christmas Eve service at church, tomorrow evening the dinner at Pamela's, and Monday was Christmas Day. She would eat Christmas Day lunch at the café in town, and time would tell as to how she would spend the rest of the day. On Tuesday morning, she would be leaving the Orange Blossom B and B Inn, bright and early.

That last thought made her sad. This little piece of

heaven had grown on her. It had such drawing power. It was beautiful—picturesque in a quaint sort of way. Idyllic was another way to describe it. She smiled as she thought about hers and Landon's synonymizing Monday night at the town café. What a hoot. What fun.

She looked about the room. Tongue-and-groove boards were on the walls as well as the ceiling, just like the rest of the interior of the little cracker gothic cottage. Pegs hung on the back of the door, and her jeans and shirts covered every one of them, and some of her clothes puddled on the floor. The floorboards attested to foot traffic through a ribbon of years, and the old-fashioned furniture was probably very near to what had been in the home originally.

What were the people like who lived here all those years ago? Landon's relatives? Ancestors, really. What were their thoughts, their feelings, their aspirations, and their goals?

She knew what her goals in life were. Her mind flitted to Phil. Funny. She hadn't thought about him all week. No, when it came to men, the only man she'd thought about was Landon. Was that bad?

"It's only natural," she said to herself, since they had spent so much time together this week. "What *is* our future? Is there even a future for us?"

She pulled on her clothing, jeans again, sleek black

ones this time, her top a bright blue crisscrossed knit. It had caught her eye in the mall, and she purchased it because of the color. She put in red, blue, and gold earrings shaped like Christmas ornaments and a matching pin on her left shoulder that played "I Saw Mommy Kissing Santa Claus" when she pressed it. It was a gift from one of the kids at church. She pressed on it now, smiling at the tinny tune. It would be sure to garner a laugh or two at the party today.

Dressed now and ready to go, she picked up her purse and dug for her keys. Landon had told her this morning when he'd brought over breakfast that he most likely wouldn't be able to make the mid-afternoon Christmas party. Another calf was about to make its entrance into the world, he'd told her.

Outside the cottage, she glanced across the road and saw no movement. That meant he wasn't going. A low feeling hit her in the gut. Her? The most upbeat of anyone around? The party person? The constantly jazzed belle of the ball? Why this sadness all of a sudden?

She got in her car, cranked up the engine, and turned on the radio. She knew the answer, as clear as the Christmas bells that jangled on the wreath on Landon's truck hood when he'd driven her around in it all week.

"A wreath on your truck?" she asked when she saw it, incredulous.

He only gave her one of his wry grins she'd come to know and like. Then he said, "Maybe some of your zaniness is rubbing off on me, Miss Zany Delaney."

She'd cackled at his nickname for her.

Then he added, "I saw another truck decorated like this, and I thought if I put a wreath on mine, I'd get a rise out of you."

"A rise?" She made her eyebrows go up and down. "This is the zaniest thing I've ever seen in my life, Mr. Bonanza." She hummed the theme song. "Dum-duh-duh-duh-duh-duh-duh-duh-duh-dum-dah. . .dum-duh-duh-duh-duh-duh-duh-duh-duh-dum-duh-duh-duh-dah." Only she was off-key, way off, and they had laughed together.

Now, as she put her car in reverse, she was immersed in her thoughts. In a few days, she would be pulling out of here, out of this enchanting man's life. That was the reason for her melancholy today. She knew it as sure as she was sitting there.

She turned the radio louder, backed up, and took off down the dirt road, her tires spinning in the ruts.

"You're just being melodramatic," she chastened herself. "Like a character in a novel." Just because she was leaving soon didn't mean that she and Landon couldn't have a relationship. A long-distance relationship was no big obstacle. In fact, she'd be willing to move to Florida in a heartbeat if there was a future for them.

She was really attracted to Landon. He seemed to be everything she was hunting for. Hunting? She smiled, thinking of their synonymizing again. When he had said "happy hunting ground," she was thinking about the fact that she was saved, single, and searching. It wasn't every day that you ran across a good man the right age who shared your faith and values, and besides that, he was as handsome as all get-out.

She remembered Uncle Rodney's and Aunt Clovis's pleas for her to graciously accept their gift of a stay at the Orange Blossom B and B.

"I believe it's providential for you to go there," Uncle Rodney had said.

"Yes," Aunt Clovis had chimed in. "I feel it in my bones, that God's got something good ahead for you, Lois."

Providential? Something good ahead? Lois turned onto the paved road and floored it as she sped down the blacktop.

Landon in her life. Landon as her. . .husband?

"That's what I want. That's what I desire."

There. She admitted it.

Would Landon become these things? Would her stay at the Orange Blossom B and B prove to be providential, as Uncle Rodney thought? Would it be the "something good ahead" Aunt Clovis felt in her bones?

Only time would tell.

And Lois was one hurry-up woman who didn't like to wait on the proverbial Father Time.

But in this case, she had no say in the matter.

❦

Phooey," Landon screeched, still waving his arms like a windmill as Lois sped off down the dirt road. "You must be doing some deep thinking, woman. You never even heard me, and I was yelling like a loon."

He dropped his arms and looked down at his white shirt that was now covered in gray dirt. He tasted grit in his mouth, felt grit in his eyes. "Phooey. I've got to go take another shower, compliments of Miss Zany Delaney." But he was smiling.

Earlier today, he'd told her he didn't think he would be able to make it to the church Christmas party. But then the calf decided to cooperate. After the birthing, Landon had rushed inside, showered, dressed, and ran out when he saw Lois get in her car. He had intended to drive them in his truck. Only it hadn't worked out that way.

He failed to get her attention, even though he'd yelled. It was a good thing he hadn't walked up behind her car, rapped on the back windshield, and barked like Marmaduke, as he first thought to do. He figured that would be a little joke on her. But she would've run right over him. Thankfully, he hadn't done that.

Now, he headed back inside his house. He would jump in the shower again, press another shirt. . . He would be late for the party, but at least he would get to attend.

# Chapter 8

Ever the cheerful one, Lois threw off her sadness like water off a duck's back as she drove down the highway. After all, tomorrow was another day. She couldn't help smiling as she thought about Scarlett O'Hara and her eternal optimism.

Within twenty minutes, she arrived at the Larsons' home. Today's party was for whomever from the church wanted to come. Pamela said there would be adults, teenagers, and children attending. It was to be a big barbecue, and she said there would be horses and ponies to ride and games for the young and old alike. She said people loved coming to the Larsons' home because they made you feel so welcome.

Rightly so. Mrs. Larson greeted Lois like she was a daughter as she stepped inside the foyer.

Pamela came across the foyer not long after Lois entered the house, carrying a silver platter of fruit. "Nice top, Lois. Looks like you dyed it to match your eyes. My friend, you're looking good today."

"Thanks. Coming from you, I consider that a compliment." Lois could see that Pamela's outfit was to die for, and besides, it revealed her womanly curves.

Pamela shrugged. "You're as cute as a button in everything you wear. Me? I'm as tall as the Tower of Babel. Want some?" She held out the fruit platter. "I'm taking this outside for Mrs. Larson, to the tables out there. That's where she's serving the food."

"Sure. I'll take a piece." Lois stabbed a wedge of fresh pineapple with a colorful toothpick.

Moments later, she greeted the pastor and his wife, then thanked them again for the lovely time she'd had at their home the past Sunday afternoon. They asked her some public relations questions, and she doled out advice freely. She was glad to help. It seemed this church was about to celebrate a major anniversary, like her church in north Georgia would soon be doing, and the pastor and his wife wanted some tips.

"When I first moved to Milton six months ago, I found out that the church would be fifty years old in one year from then. The first thing I did was form a committee to plan a month's worth of events for the anniversary month. I also planned one event for each month leading up to it. Next, I made the newspaper aware of our plans. They're doing an article a month on us. That's pretty groovy. Free advertising."

She was sure her eyes were showing her excitement. She always got excited talking about PR, especially when it furthered the kingdom of God. "Then, I started a children's program on Sunday mornings. If you want to reach young families, you'd better have a hopping kids' program. Our church was considered an older congregation—"

"The congregation got older through the years," the pastor said, "and no young families were added, right?"

"Right. When our community suddenly realized that Christ Church was on the map via the newspaper articles, and, coupling that with the new kids' program, well, our attendance started growing by leaps and bounds. I'm training workers now so that when I leave, they can take over." She had already explained to the pastor and his wife that her church secretary stint was temporary.

"Why don't you come work for us?" the pastor asked. "We can't pay you what a big firm in Atlanta could. But we'd make it worth your while—eventually. We're a small church, but we have big dreams."

Lois was dumbfounded. Just this very morning, she had decided that if there was a future for her and Landon, she would move to Florida in a heartbeat.

"Think about it, okay?"

"Okay."

For an hour, Lois wandered inside and out. She watched the children riding the horses and ponies. She stopped at the booths and tried her hand, taking her turn standing in line with kids and adults alike.

The beanbag throw. The ball roll across the lawn. The bean drop in three different sized cans. The Ping-Pong ball toss. The red-and-green-candy-in-the-jar guess. The puzzle puzzler.

The seed-spitting contest?

"Step right up, Miss," said the elderly man at the booth. "See how far you can spit a seed."

Lois laughed, imagining herself taking aim with her mouth and hurling a seed through the air. She might be silly but she wasn't crazy. Spitting seeds the farthest? No thanks.

"Can you make it two feet?" he said. "Three feet? Four?"

She smiled. "I'll pass, thank you."

Pamela came to her side, as well as a few other singles, from the college-aged to senior citizens, the same ones who'd been at the pastor's house last week. "Lois, Lois," they chanted over and over. "Lois, Lois, she's our man, if she can't do it, nobody can." They said the cheerleader cheer until a crowd gathered.

After much coaxing and amidst much laughter, Lois stepped up to the line.

"Get yerself a seed," the elderly man said.

On a small table, Lois saw a plastic butter tub filled with some sort of seeds. "Are these recycled seeds?" she joked.

"Not that I know of." His eyes twinkled. "I was told they're pumpkin seeds. Mrs. Larson carved the pumpkin herself, and she's got the pies to prove it."

Warily, Lois reached down, retrieved one of the seeds from the tub, and took a runner's stance, her right toe on the line.

The singles around her chanted her name again. "Lois-Lois-Lois-Lois."

Lois put the seed in her mouth. "Shoo-wee." She scrunched up her nose. "These things are salty." She pursed her lips, taking aim.

"Get ready," the elderly man said. "Get set. Go."

She thrust her head forward, spit the seed with all her might, and didn't even see where it landed because the grass was sparse and the seed was the color of the dirt.

The elderly man found her seed on the ground, marked it with a tall stick, and congratulated her for her distance, as did the others gathered around.

*I sure am glad Landon isn't here.* She didn't mind being the instigator of silliness, but this took the cake.

Landon spotted Lois in the food line and made his way to her. "Nice spitting, Lois," he whispered, grinning.

She whipped around, her plate of food nearly toppling out of her hands. "You startled me." She looked shy, embarrassed even. "I thought you weren't going to come? I thought you said you wouldn't be able to make it? Uh. How long have you been here?" Her questions tumbled out staccato-like as she clutched at her throat.

"Long enough. I saw the contest." He wouldn't tell her that he had also entered it after she walked away. "The calf made her debut earlier than I expected, and so I was able to come. Why? Are you sorry?" He chuckled, envisioning her in the seed-spitting contest.

She smiled at him, genuine warmth in her eyes this time. "Oh, no. I—I'm glad you came. It's just that as I was. . .spitting that. . .that stupid seed, I was saying to myself that I sure was glad you weren't around. Now, I'm finding out you were there watching."

"Like I said, nice spitting, Lois. Your lips must have some strong pucker power."

Her face turned as red as the barbecue sauce on her plate. "I—I. . ."

"No need to get flustered." He patted her arm, grinning, amused as all get-out. And attracted, too, very attracted to her. He felt that spark again, what he'd felt the first night they met.

"I–I. . ." Her voice trailed off. It was so unlike her to be at a loss for words.

Liking what he felt about her, getting flustered himself, he turned quickly, toward the food line. "I'm going to get some barbecue. Save me a seat at your table, okay?"

∾✶∾

Late that afternoon at the Larsons' home, everyone—adults and children alike—gathered their lawn chairs in a wide-spreading cluster. Lois found herself sandwiched between Landon and Pamela.

The pastor led in singing Christmas carols. That was followed by testimonies offered spontaneously by people who attested to God's goodness in their lives in the past year. Then the pastor brought a Christmas devotional.

Lois enjoyed the warm camaraderie, her heart touched by everyone's kindness and friendship.

The woman who was in charge of the games stood and came to the front of the group. "I'd like to announce the winners of the various contests. We have some prizes to hand out. Drumroll, please."

Everybody beat on the armrests of their lawn chairs, the palm-to-aluminum *thwacks* making everyone laugh as the woman set prizes on a card table in front of her.

Landon seemed to be in a playful mood. He leaned over and thwacked Lois's armrest a few times, and she did the same thing to his.

The woman picked up a prize off the table. "The children's winner of the beanbag throw is Chase Miller."

The crowd clapped as little Chase came forward to claim her prize, a red net Christmas stocking filled to the brim with Christmas candy.

"The adult winner of the beanbag throw is Marta Johnson."

The crowd clapped as Marta came forward and received an identical prize.

"The children's winner of the Ping-Pong ball toss is Cassidy Kelly."

The crowd clapped as little Cassidy came forward and received her prize.

On and on the woman went, calling out the winners in both the children's and adult categories, awarding the prizes, the crowd clapping.

"And now, for the seed-spitting contest, we'll announce the adult category first. We've divided it into two parts. Men and women. Ladies first. The winner for the women's division is"—she thrust out her hand dramatically—"drumroll, please"—everybody thwacked on their armrests—"Lois Delaney."

The crowd cheered uproariously.

Lois, feeling the heat rise to her face, got up and made her way to the front.

"And the winner of the men's division"—the woman thrust out her hand dramatically—"again, drumroll, please"—everybody thwacked on their armrests—"is Landon Michael."

Landon made his way to the front and grinned his disarming grin at Lois, which made her heart beat all the harder. He took his place by her side as the crowd made playful catcalls and clapped loudly.

"The prize for this important contest is, tah-dah—a pumpkin." From under the table, the woman drew out two orange pillows in the shape of pumpkins. "Well, they're pumpkin pillows. I'm sure they'll remind you of this day for a long time." She held them out in front of her. "Lois and Landon, we hereby proclaim you the champion seed-spitters of our entire congregation. Congratulations!"

Applause broke out again.

Landon leaned close to Lois. "The secret's in the lips." Then he winked at her.

Lois couldn't think of a thing to whisper back, not a thing.

❦

On her way home from the Christmas party, Lois pressed her Christmas pin on her left shoulder, the tinny tune filling the car. "I Saw Mommy Kissing Santa Claus." She sang along.

Then she pressed it again and sang along, only she changed the words.

"I *felt Landon* kissing *Loi—is*," she sang softly over and over.

# Chapter 9

Standing on the church steps after Christmas Eve service, Landon asked Lois to ride with him to Pamela's home for Christmas Eve dinner that evening.

"Thanks, it'll save gas," she told him.

He rolled his eyes out of her view. Sometimes her thriftiness annoyed him. Oh, it wasn't that he was loaded. He gave reasonable attention to his finances. He just didn't squeeze the dollars as much as she did. He'd had a lifetime doing that as a minister's son, and that was enough.

That evening, as they rode down the highway, he wasn't thinking about her penny-pinching ways that sort of irked him. He was thinking about how good she smelled, and how energized she was, and how nice she looked. Tonight, it was crisply pressed black jeans, high-heeled black boots, and another top that matched those mesmerizing blue eyes of hers. She chattered about this and that, apparently content to let him sit quietly not saying much, just enjoying her company. That was a nice feeling, not to be pressured to join in a conversation, and it pleased him that she allowed him to do this.

He marveled at her. She was as smart as a whip, always coming up with ideas. Right now, she was talking about how he could promote the Orange Blossom B and B as a place for brides to bring their bridesmaids the weekend before their weddings for a bride's slumber party. Nifty idea, if he said so himself.

"You could even have weddings in the orange grove." She turned toward him, her face awash with excitement. "You could advertise them as 'A Wedding Beneath the Blossoms.' The bride and her bridesmaids could get dressed in the cracker cottage. The receptions could be held under big white tents, or in town somewhere."

He smiled and nodded as she continued talking, suggesting that he also promote the B and B as a place for small family reunions. Small tents could be put up in the backyard for the kids to sleep in, she said. Kids would love that, she went on, cousins camping out with cousins.

"Groovy." He laughed as he said the old-fashioned word she was always using. "I can see why you won awards in the public relations field. You're very clever."

"Thanks."

He leaned forward and tuned the radio to Christmas carols. "Silent Night" wafted through the car. "The Christmas Eve service this morning was meaningful, don't you think?"

She ran her hand through her bouncy blond hair and turned toward him. "Very touching. The children's number added a special touch, and then, when the choir sang the 'Hallelujah Chorus'—why I felt like shouting, 'Hallelujah!'"

"You mean you wouldn't have said yee-haw?" He chuckled.

"I–I. . .when did you. . . ?" She clutched at her throat.

He loved it when the cat got her tongue. That had to be a mighty big cat, because she loved to talk. He smiled inwardly, envisioning a big, fat tabby. "When did I hear you say yee-haw?"

She nodded, still clutching her throat, looking like a kid with her hand caught in the cookie jar.

He loved it when she got shy. He didn't know why. But it attracted him to her like a bee to a blossom. He chuckled again. "It was the first morning you were here. I'd just put your breakfast in the kitchen. I went around back to get some logs, and I was coming down the side of the cottage when I heard you holler 'Yee-haw!'"

"I had no idea you were around. . . ."

"Just like when you were spitting seeds?"

She looked down, fiddled with her purse at her side, and didn't say anything.

With a sidelong glance her way, in the dimness of the dashboard lights he saw her thick eyelashes sweeping her cherry-red cheeks. He resisted the urge to reach over and caress those cherry-red cheeks. Innocence. That's why he liked her shyness. It showed her innocence, and he loved that about her. Loved? He bit his bottom lip, thinking hard.

Finally, she spoke, softly. "Yee-haw is a word I use when there's no other word to describe the joy I'm feeling. It's *really* zany, so I never say it in front of anyone."

After that, neither said a word for miles. They rode down the dark highway in the car that was lit up only by dashboard lights, both of them apparently lost in thought. When they approached town, he noticed the red and green reindeer-shaped lights that hung from tall light poles. On one street corner was a group singing Christmas carols.

"So you liked our choir's rendition of the 'Hallelujah Chorus' this morning?" Landon stopped at a traffic light, humming "We Wish You a Merry Christmas" along with the carolers on the corner.

"Oh, yes. I haven't seen a choir do that in a long time.

I'll have to suggest that to Uncle Rodney for our church next year. I thought a choir had to have a lot more voices to pull that off, but I see now that even a smaller church can do justice to the 'Hallelujah Chorus.' When I lived in Atlanta, I went to a huge church, and we had a hundred-voice choir." She paused, like she was in deep contemplation. "That church was great, but there's something special about smaller congregations, don't you think? I never knew that until I started working with Uncle Rodney."

*So much for her shyness,* he thought with a wry grin.

"I have lots to tell Uncle Rodney when I get home. Suggestions to make, and all."

"Here we are." Landon turned into Pamela's driveway. Her house was nearly identical to every house lining the street, except that her Christmas decorations were tasteful.

"Groovy decorations." Lois picked up her purse.

He turned off the ignition. "Pamela decorated the inside of her home nicely, too."

"You've been here?" Her eyebrows arched.

"She—"

"I'm sorry. I shouldn't have asked that. It's none of my business."

"Pamela hosted a get-together for the church singles group."

"Oh."

He wouldn't tell her that Pamela had also had him for dinner twice during the first two weeks of December. When she invited him the third time, he was tied up. And the fourth time. And the fifth. She hadn't asked since then.

"I've only known Pamela a week, but I'm sure we'll be friends for life. Ever heard that song? It's old, I know. It was popular when I was a teenager." She clasped her hands together dramatically. "Friends are friends forever," she belted out, "if the Lord's the Lord of them. . ."

He winced. What an off-key voice she had, and apparently she didn't care.

She laughed her bright, hyena-like laugh. "I'm being silly, aren't I? I get this way when I'm excited." Her feet pitter-pattered on the floorboard. "Christmas Day is tomorrow!" She reached for her door handle.

"I'll get your door." He opened his door, climbed out of the car, shut the door behind him, and walked to the passenger side. He opened her door, held it while she climbed out. He touched her elbow, guiding her up the walk. The moment he had touched her, there was that spark again.

All the way to Pamela's front door, he hummed inwardly. But it wasn't "We Wish You a Merry Christmas." It was a golden oldie his grandfather used to sing.

"Let Me Call You Sweetheart."

❧

When Lois and Landon stepped inside Pamela's home,

she greeted them both warmly, Southern hospitality exuding from her.

Everywhere Lois looked, she saw Pamela's flair for entertaining, from the cinnamon scents that beckoned, to the tall Scotch pine that shimmered, to the Christmas carols that soothed, to the luscious hors d'oeuvres that set her taste buds watering.

"Oh, Pamela," she exclaimed, looking at the tree bedecked with gold and silver ornaments and hundreds of tiny white lights. "It's the most stunning Christmas tree I've ever seen."

"Thank you, Lois." Pamela stood looking at the tall tree. "I love Christmas. It's my favorite time of all. The decorating and cooking and baking and gift buying. . . why, it's the most wonderful time of the year."

Lois sauntered to the mantel that was strung with greenery, spellbound. The greenery sported the same gold and silver decorations as the tree. "Everything is beautiful."

Pamela looked pleased.

Lois glanced around the room. Over a large archway were the same greenery and decorations. The coffee table had a similar floral arrangement. Through the archway, she saw the dining table adorned with yet another arrangement of like fashion. Everything coordinated. "What magic you work with your hands, Pamela."

"What a nice thing to say."

Lois grabbed Pamela in a sisterly hug, and they both laughed.

"Let's get started with some finger foods, shall we?" Pamela made her way across the room.

"Sounds good to me." Lois was close on Pamela's heels.

"I made some of Landon's favorites tonight." Pamela stopped at a marble-topped chest. Pointing at the small silver trays containing hors d'oeuvres, she motioned for Landon to come.

Lois smiled at Landon as he approached. "You're so quiet, I almost forgot you were here."

"I didn't." Pamela gave Landon a dazzling smile.

Landon joined them where they stood near the marble-topped chest.

"I made shrimp dip for you, Landon." Pamela seemed to have eyes only for Landon.

A twinge of jealousy hit Lois. It was now obvious to her that Pamela had her dibs on Landon. Twenty minutes ago, in the car, she had told Landon what a great friend Pamela was. *So much for my talkativeness. Why couldn't I keep my big mouth shut for once?*

But then another thought hit her, one of contrition for feeling jealousy in the first place. Landon was an open playing field. She had no claim on him. And besides,

Christians weren't supposed to be jealous.

"Here, Landon." Pamela held out a shrimp-dip-laden cracker on a napkin. "I know you love this stuff." She had a playful look about her, her eyes lighting up like the Christmas lights behind her.

He took the cracker from her. "One of my favorites, as you said, Pamela." He popped it in his mouth. "Delicious." He rubbed his midsection.

"Here, Lois." Pamela held out a cracker on a napkin to Lois.

"Thanks." Lois took it and nibbled it. "Yes, it's delicious." Her manner was stilted. She couldn't help it.

All through Pamela's exquisite dinner of stuffed Cornish hens, potatoes au gratin, and fresh asparagus with hollandaise sauce, Lois was quieter than usual. She could never hope to compare with Pamela. The woman was a wonder in all that mattered to a man.

After they ate their dessert—trifle in a footed glass bowl—the evening came to an end, and Lois was glad. Lois and Landon said their adieus and left.

As Landon drove toward home, Lois didn't say too much. She had a whole lot of thinking to do.

❧

*What's up with Lois?* Landon couldn't help wondering as he drove down the highway. *She chatters like a magpie all the way to Pamela's, and she's as quiet as a clam all the way home.*

Had he done something to offend her? He certainly had not. Did she think he had flirted with Pamela? He certainly had not. He couldn't help it that the woman was on the prowl. Oh, he didn't mean that like it sounded. Pamela was a nice enough young woman. And he knew Lois really liked her. She'd said so on the way there.

When they'd arrived, Lois was as friendly as all get-out. She went on and on about Pamela's decorating, even hugged her like a sister while she laughed like a hyena. Miss Zany Delaney. But after that, Lois grew quiet, and she was still acting that way now.

He thought about Pamela again. She'd come on strong all evening, like she was staking her claim on him. Had she been trying to get a subtle message across to Lois? Most decidedly so. In fact, there was nothing subtle about it. He knew what was going on. He wasn't born yesterday. Pamela was in pursuit. And Lois was in retreat.

He had quickly grown weary of the cutesy romantic triangle they had thrust upon him all evening. . .Miss Perky Pamela, overextending herself to him at every turn. . .

Miss Languid Lois, withdrawn and out of sorts. . .

And him? He was Mr. Lame Landon, ever the gentleman, trying to keep peace.

*Women,* he fumed inwardly. *All they think about is the M word.*

"Phooey." He thumped the steering wheel.

"Did you leave something at Pamela's?" Lois glanced his way. "Your jacket? You don't have it on."

"It's in the backseat."

"Oh."

He slowed for the turnoff to his road. Tomorrow was Christmas Day. Lois had told him she had enjoyed some times of quiet reflection while at the Orange Blossom. Well, tomorrow he would take all day for his own quiet reflection.

He would put the turkey in the oven. Though he wasn't a cook—a few breakfast foods were his limits—surely he could bake a turkey. He would follow the directions on the wrapper. It was that simple. And he would cook some rice—no, he couldn't make turkey gravy so it would have to be mashed potatoes. Mashed potatoes tasted better without gravy than rice did. And he would open a can of green beans.

All the while he was preparing his meal, and then during the eating of it, he would quietly reflect. Maybe he would find some of that refreshment Lois talked about. And revitalization. And rejuvenation.

He surely hoped so.

❧

Lois didn't know what to think, so she tried not to. As the miles ticked off, she sat there just like Landon, not saying a word. It certainly wasn't like this on the way. She had been so excited that she talked up a storm. Now, she felt numb.

But her thoughts started whirling again, even though she was trying hard not to think.

She reflected on how quiet a guy Landon was. At times, she wished he would enter into conversations with her. And why had he acted that way all evening? Like a lame duck was how she would describe him.

And why had Pamela been like that? So solicitous of him that it made Lois want to scream. When Lois walked in, her first thought had been how gracious and hospitable Pamela was. Within five minutes, Lois knew Pamela for what she was. A woman with a mission. To get Landon Michael.

A cold chill hit Lois. Wasn't that what she was, too? A woman with a mission? To get Landon Michael? Just the other day she'd admitted to herself that she wanted Landon in her life, particularly as a husband. Then what was the difference between her and Pamela? They clearly wanted the same thing.

Lois shifted in her seat in Landon's car. She'd never felt so down. Though Landon was five inches from her, it felt like five miles. And it might as well be.

She glanced over at him. His eyes were narrowed, and his mouth was in a thin line. He looked contemplative—no, contemptuous was more like it.

He probably had her pegged—a woman just like Pamela. And he probably felt she was a loony toon with her loud, boisterous ways in comparison to his solemnity. Loony-toon Lois. A fitting name.

Well, one more day and she would be out of here. And that meant out of his life. Forever.

He would probably like that.

She pushed down the sob that threatened to gurgle up her throat.

# Chapter 10

Christmas morning, Landon pulled the thawed turkey out of the refrigerator and set it in the sink. He studied the directions on the plastic packaging. If he got it in the oven now, he could eat Christmas dinner at one o'clock or so.

"I should invite Lois." He glanced out the windows at the cottage across the road. "She's all alone, and nobody should be alone for Christmas."

"I'm eating with Alberta on Christmas Day," she had told him when he dropped her off last night. "The café's open for the midday Christmas meal."

He thought of his own Christmas plans today, eating and quietly reflecting. Then he thought about his original plans, before he booked Lois at the B and B. It was his annual custom to drive to his parents' parsonage in

North Carolina and spend a few days with them during the holiday season.

Tomorrow morning, as soon as Lois left, he would head up there. His parents had been understanding when he told them about his delay. His father, just as he expected, had been amused about the unusual booking by the preacher in north Georgia for his church secretary.

"Unusual booking? Unusual lady." Landon couldn't get his mind off Lois this morning. How did he feel about her? Was there a chance of a future for them? He thought about their differences.

Her, the talker; him, the quiet one.

Her, the disorganized; him, the neatnik.

Her, the spendthrift; him, the spender.

But then he thought about their commonalities.

Their faith.

Their values.

Their morals.

And he reflected on her little snippets of shyness that intrigued him. He remembered her lovingkindness to everyone she met.

"Yes, I'll invite her to eat Christmas dinner with me."

As he cut the packaging off the turkey, then scissored around the cooking directions and laid the small plastic square on the counter, his earlier questions gnawed at him. *How do I feel about her? Is there a chance of a future for us?*

He shrugged his shoulders. "I'll take her carefree, que sera sera attitude concerning our future. What will be, will be."

He put the turkey in the oven, walked across the road to the cottage, and knocked on the front door.

❦

After Lois ate the breakfast Landon laid out for her, she pulled out her Bible. She turned to Psalm 37:4–6, the passage she had reflected on all week.

"Delight yourself in the Lord and he will give you the desires of your heart," she read. "Commit your way to the Lord; trust in him and he will do this: He will make your righteousness shine like the dawn, the justice of your cause like the noonday sun."

She ran her hand across the sacrosanct words, then looked heavenward. "Okay, Lord, I've been delighting in You. Now, I'm going to commit my way to You. I desire Landon really bad. He's so groovy. I think the teenagers at church would say he's one awesome hottie. But if he's not the one You have for me, then. . .then close the door."

Her heart pounded. Those words were hard—no, torturous—to say. "I. . .I commit him. . .as well as the future of our relationship. . .into Your hands, dear Jesus."

*Keep trusting in Me,* the Lord seemed to whisper.

"Okay, Lord, I'll do that. I'll trust You. And I know You'll do Your part, as it says in the Word. You're going to make my righteousness shine like the dawn, and the justice of my cause like the noonday sun, whatever that means for me."

She drummed her fingers on the table. "What explanation did the pastor give for the last part of that passage? Hmm. Now I remember. He said it means that God will answer our prayers, He will vindicate us, and He will give us guidance."

She bowed her head. "Lord, first I'm asking You to answer my prayers, namely, to help me put You first in my life no matter what happens in my *love* life. Second, I'm asking You to vindicate me. I feel like such a goon around Landon. Sometimes I get excited, and I feel that he gets annoyed about it. Help him to see me as I truly am, a woman with a heart after You. Third, I'm asking You to give me guidance. I don't know what the future holds. But You do, Lord. You know my right hand from my left. You know the number of hairs on my head. So lead me now, dear Jesus. In Thy name I pray. Amen."

*Knock-knock.*

Lois looked up. Who could that be? Landon was the only likely caller. Why was he over here? She got up from the table and pulled the sash of her robe more tightly about her waist. She walked to the front door and opened it a crack, just enough to see out. After all, she was in her robe. There stood Landon, as she expected.

But again, why was he here?

"Earth to Lois." He laughed. "You there?"

She smiled, feeling shy.

"Merry Christmas." He jangled a silver bell at her.

"Same to you."

"Can you come to my house for Christmas dinner?"

"Alberta's cooking dinner for me, in town—"

"I know Alberta's cooking. But I'm cooking, too. And I'd like you to join me, if you will. I can't cook like Alberta, but hopefully it'll be fit to eat."

"I wouldn't want to—"

"Discombobulate me?" He chuckled.

She laughed. "You remembered that funny, old-fashioned word my great-grandmother would've used?"

He nodded. "I just put the turkey in the oven. It should be ready by one o'clock. Say you'll come. There's no way I can eat a whole turkey by myself."

She stood there thinking. He really sounded like he wanted her to come. That made her feel good. Maybe he didn't think she was a complete ignoramus. Perhaps there was hope for them after all.

He held the silver bell higher, jangling it again. "Lois?"

"All right. I'll be there at one. And thanks for the invitation. I'm sure it'll be delicious."

Ten minutes later, she was in the shower, deep in

thought. A poem formed in her mind, and she said it aloud.

> *I hope I can act*
> *Dignified today.*
> *Maybe he'll like me*
> *Better that way.*

She cackled at her silly little rhyme. But in her heart, she hoped it came true.

# Chapter 11

Landon felt bad as he looked over the burnt part of the turkey, toward Lois where she sat on the other side of his dining room table. The top part of the bird was as black as tar and smelled almost as bad.

"So much for reading directions. I thought sure I could cook a turkey."

"You win some, you lose some." She smiled at him, empathy in her eyes. "I'm sure it'll taste good."

He shrugged. "I shouldn't have run out to the barn when I did. I thought I'd only be out there a few minutes, but then I got dirty, and then I had to take another shower, and while I was in the shower, the smoke started, and of course I couldn't see it, had no idea the turkey was burning—"

"You sound like me." She looked up at him shyly.

"Talking so much and all?"

"No, I was thinking about our cooking skills. Or should I say, lack thereof?"

He smiled at her. "Shall we pray?"

Throughout dinner, their conversation proceeded without a hitch. Landon was glad. What with the burnt turkey and the undercooked mashed potatoes, he needed something pleasant going on. Lois talked in her usual bright, cheerful way, though he noticed she was somewhat subdued. He was his normal self. Quiet but with a listening ear.

She helped him clean the kitchen, which was nice. He wondered why he had cooked today—or attempted to, he should say. He should've gone to the café, like Lois had planned to do.

He scraped the plates. She loaded the dishes in the dishwasher. He washed the platters and the pots. She dried them. He put them away. He. She. He. She. He. She. They seemed to work well together. That was a pleasant thought to him as they finished in the kitchen.

"Will you excuse me for a moment while I call Aunt Clovis and Uncle Rodney and wish them a merry Christmas?" She picked up her purse from the sofa, reached inside it, and pulled out her cell phone.

"Sure."

She dialed a number.

"While you do that, I'm going to the barn. I'll be back in a few minutes, okay?"

The phone to her ear, she mouthed, "Okay."

Fifteen minutes later, when he came back inside, she was in the kitchen, looking in his cabinets.

She turned, her hand on a cabinet knob, her cheeks cherry red. "I–I. . ."

He smiled. There it was again. That shy, innocent look about her.

She found her voice. "Aunt Clovis said I should make you a dessert. I was looking for cookbooks. But I don't want to be presump—"

"Please proceed. A dessert sounds wonderful. Look in the cabinet over the phone. I think you'll find a few cookbooks in there." He walked toward his recliner in the adjacent great room and sat down. "While you do that, mind if I look at the sports channel for a few minutes?"

⁂

Lois opened the cabinet door over the phone, saw a shelf full of cookbooks. One caught her eye. *Delightfully Southern Recipes* by Lucy M. Clark.

Excited, she pulled it out, read a little, found it was written by a Georgia author—yes!—turned to the index, and on a lark looked up the word "orange." To her delight, she saw eleven recipes. When she spotted Orange Blossoms, she almost did a joy jig. She flipped to the page and read the recipe. It looked easy enough.

"Do you have any cake mixes, Landon?" She projected her voice across the wide kitchen bar.

"You can look in the pantry, but I don't think so."

She opened the pantry door and scanned the shelves. "Rats." She whipped out her cell phone and dialed Aunt Clovis again. "Aunt Clovis, do you have an easy recipe for a yellow cake?"

"Why? Did you decide to make Mr. Landon Michael"—she cackled like Lois was always doing—"imagine a name like that." Her laughter trailed off. "Did you decide to make him a dessert, darlin'?"

"Yes, ma'am. I'm making Orange Blossoms. You pour yellow cake batter into miniature muffin tins, bake them, and then dip them in an orange glaze. Yum, yum. And it's so apropos, too." Lois smiled one of Landon's wry grins as she looked out the windows. "We're surrounded with orange blossoms, you know."

"Yes, darlin'," Aunt Clovis said in her Georgia twang. "I saw them pictures in the magazine, remember."

"This recipe I found looks luscious, Aunt Clovis. But it says you have to have a cake mix, and I don't have one. So I thought I'd use a substitute. An easy yellow cake recipe is what I was thinking."

"Have no fear, the chef is here. Hold on, darlin,' while I get my recipe box."

Lois heard fumbling on the end of the line as she waited.

"Here it is. It's called 1-2-3-4 cake. It's as easy as pie."

Lois jotted down the recipe as Aunt Clovis dictated it. Then she told her good-bye and hung up.

"Landon," she called across the wide bar, "I'm making you some orange blossoms."

"Orange blossoms?"

"They're little cake-like thingies with an orange glaze."

"Do I have the ingredients? I don't know of a store that's open on Christmas Day. Even the mini-mart."

"Hmm. Aunt Clovis's cake recipe is pretty basic. Butter, sugar, flour, eggs—that sort of thing. You have those?"

"I think so." He got to his feet, came in the kitchen, and helped her gather the ingredients onto the counter.

"I'm not much of a cook," she told him, "but both of these recipes—Aunt Clovis's and this Lucy M. Clark's—look like a cinch. Any dimwit can make Orange Blossoms."

❦

Landon stretched out in his recliner, the TV tuned to a sports channel, a fire going in the hearth, the AC cranked up to high, the pleasant sounds of a woman working in his kitchen sounding like music to his ears.

❦

Lois's hands shook. She wanted these luscious little orange thingies to turn out well for Landon. She looked in a bottom cabinet for miniature muffin tins. Only round cake pans. Rats. She looked in the next cabinet, then the next. None anywhere. Oh well, who cared? She would make a two-layer cake and pour the luscious orange glaze all over it.

Butter, sugar, baking powder, eggs, flour, milk, vanilla flavoring. She sifted the dry stuff together, then combined the wet stuff, according to Aunt Clovis's recipe. *This is as simple as 1-2-3-4, just like the cake's name.*

She would've hummed, but she saw that Landon's eyes were closed where he lay in his recliner. *He must've dozed off.*

Carefully, she poured the batter into the two cake pans and set them in the preheated oven. *Tah-dah, I even remembered to turn the oven on, heh-heh-heh.* Then she turned the timer on.

She whipped up the orange glaze, set it aside, and joined Landon in the great room, delicious smells already scenting the air. A quick glance his way told her he was still dozing. She took a seat on the sofa, being careful not to awaken him, though she was itching to talk.

*Nothing says lovin' like something from the oven,* she hummed inwardly, the Pillsbury ditty filling her heart. She smiled, feeling like a kid finding a pony on Christmas morning.

Shortly, the timer dinged.

"I smell something good." Landon opened his eyes and pushed the recliner forward. "Yum, yum, as you're always saying."

"Yum, yum is right." She jumped up from the sofa and made her way into the kitchen. She pulled open the oven door, leaned down, and peered at the cake pans.

She let out a wail, couldn't help it.

"What's wrong?" Landon came running into the kitchen, alarm in his voice.

She let out another wail.

"Burn yourself?" He was behind her now.

She stood there, staring at the cake pans in the oven.

He bent down and looked at them. He stood up, laughing like she was always doing—like a hyena. He laughed so hard, tears watered his eyes.

She stood there in shock.

He finally quit laughing. "What did you do to that cake?"

She pulled out the two cake pans with oven mitts and set them on a protective mat.

He started laughing again.

She looked down at two little pancake-like cakes, one in each pan. The pans should've been filled with delicious yellow cake by now. "I guess I. . .I. . . ." She went over a mental checklist of ingredients, remembering each one. "I guess I forgot to add something. . . ." She spotted the sack of flour by the sink and felt deflated—no, embarrassed beyond words.

His gaze followed hers, and he was laughing again, uproariously. "Lois, you forgot the flour."

❦

Landon watched Lois cross the road and enter the cottage.

He started laughing again and couldn't seem to quit. He'd never laughed this hard in all his life.

"To forget the flour? That takes the cake!"

He laughed at his pun.

"Any dimwit can make Orange Blossoms," she'd said.

As he scraped the orange glaze out of the mixing bowl and washed it down the sink drain—he'd insisted on cleaning up the kitchen—his burnt turkey came to mind.

"Well, Lois, we have another thing in common. Neither one of us can cook." He licked a dollop of orange glaze off the spoon, then chuckled. "No, we can't cook a lick."

# Chapter 12

That evening, Landon looked outside the windows of his great room. Though there was no moon and the sky was as black as velvet, the night was young. He made his way outside, picked up a lantern on the porch, unleashed Marmaduke, and headed for the orange grove.

In a clearing, he sat on a bench, told Marmaduke to sit, set the lantern on the ground in front of him. He would do some of that quiet reflecting, what he hadn't had time to do all day. First, he had cooked Christmas dinner. Then he and Lois ate together. Then there was the cake mistake.

"Cake mistake? I'm pretty clever, if I do say so myself." He chuckled.

After the cake mistake, she had left, and the afternoon

whiled away with him getting another leisurely, restful nap. "Now, for some quiet reflection."

Immediately, Lois popped into his mind. . . .

Lois with her cheerfulness.

Lois with her humor.

Lois with her kindness.

Lois with her devotion to God.

Lois, Lois, Lois.

It seemed he couldn't get his thoughts to focus elsewhere.

*Lord, give me guidance concerning her.*

Marmaduke growled.

"Easy, boy." He looked through the orange grove and saw a thin trail of light coming his way. A flashlight? Lois, perhaps? Of course. It couldn't be anyone else.

Marmaduke barked.

The thin trail of light went in the opposite direction.

"Lois? Is that you?"

The thin trail of light halted.

"Lois? If it's you, please come toward my lantern."

The thin trail of light proceeded toward him. In moments, she was in front of him. "I'm sorry. I didn't mean to disturb you."

He patted the spot beside him. "Have a seat?"

She hesitated.

"Please? I'd like to talk to you. Something I don't do

much of, as you've probably noticed." He smiled up at her.

She took tentative steps toward him, then sat next to him.

He took the flashlight out of her hands and turned it off. The moment their hands touched, he felt the spark. In that instant, he knew that he knew.

*She's the woman for me.*

*Thank You, Lord.*

"You're sure quiet tonight, Lois." The lantern on the ground gave off the perfect amount of light, dim and romantic.

"Reflecting, that's all." Her voice was soft.

"Me, too. That's why I came out here. I was reflecting on our relationship."

She didn't respond.

He breathed in the night air, thick with the scent of orange blossoms all about them. He laughed, thinking about her Orange Blossom recipe. Thingies, she'd called them. "I was laughing because I was thinking that you cook about as well as I do."

She let out a gentle laugh.

He wanted to put his arms around her, hug her to him and tell her what she meant to him. He would start slowly.

She breathed in deeply, like she was enjoying the scent of the orange blossoms, too.

"I'm a little old-fashioned, just like my cracker gothic

cottage." He grinned. "So I'll ask you before I attempt it. May I hold your hand?"

She nodded as she looked down and fiddled with her bracelet.

He studied her. If the sun were shining, he was sure her cheeks would be cherry red, and the thought thrilled him. He reached out, found her hand, clasped it in his, and squeezed it.

She squeezed back.

"A few minutes ago, I was praying for guidance." *Concerning you.*

"I–I prayed for that, too, this morning," she whispered.

His heart rejoiced. There was that telltale catch in her voice. "And what did the Lord say to you?"

"He told me to keep trusting Him." Quietly and concisely, she explained the passage in the Bible she'd been reflecting on all week. "Those verses became my guidepost in matters that. . .well, that apply to. . .me."

He drew in a lungful of the scented air as he gathered her in his arms and hugged her to him. "You know what I think?"

"What?"

"I think that. . .love is a-bloom."

"I–I think. . .so, too."

❧

Early the next morning, Lois loaded her car, her heart

feeling as light as a feather after what happened last night.

She recalled how he had asked to hold her hand. "I'm a little old-fashioned," he'd said. She was, too, but she was so overjoyed at his romantic overture, she felt like saying, *Forget the old-fashioned stuff. Just take me in your arms, mister.* She smiled at the thought.

Now, Landon crossed the road and came toward her. "Since I'm heading for North Carolina, and you're heading for north Georgia, what about if I followed along behind you on I-75? We could stop for meals together, all day long."

"Sounds like a great idea." She flashed him a brilliant smile, her heart beating hard.

His eyebrows raised. "Not groovy?"

"Well, that, too."

He put his arms around her. "*This* sounds like a great idea. Groovy, too." He hugged her tightly.

She smiled, wanting to do a joy jig but restraining herself. Instead, she hugged him back warmly.

"Ahh, Lois. . ."

"Landon. . ."

He drew back and stared down into her eyes.

She thought her heart would melt.

"I'd like to conduct an experiment." His voice was husky.

"Experiment?" All she could think of were the test tubes she saw in his high school chemistry lab when he'd given her a tour of the building.

"I'd like to test your pucker power. . . ."

Feeling shy, she averted her eyes.

He cupped her chin and lifted her face. Their eyes met. He came toward her, lips meeting lips. For a long moment, they stood in the sunshine surrounded by a heavenly fragrance, entwined in a sweet embrace.

He released her, seemingly out of breath. His eyes were playful as he looked into hers. "I'm at a loss for words. But that's not unusual. Do you have anything to say?" His chest heaved as he waited.

"Yee-haw!"

# ORANGE BLOSSOMS
## by Lucy M. Clarke

Duncan Hines Golden Butter Cake Mix

1) Set oven at 350 degrees.
2) Make cake mix according to directions but add 1 tsp. orange extract.
3) Spray miniature muffin tins with Pam and fill ⅔ full.
4) Bake until just barely browned. Tip: This takes very little time in the oven, so keep a close watch. The goal is for them to be moist.

Glaze
2 cups powdered sugar
1 tsp. finely shredded orange peel (optional)
enough orange juice to make a runny glaze

1) Mix ingredients together.
2) Dip each muffin in glaze and place on rack to harden.
3) Enjoy! Yum, yum!

# ORANGE-PECAN CAKE
## by Sharon Schuller Kiser

½ cup chopped pecans
⅔ cup butter, softened
1½ cups sugar
3 eggs, separated
¾ cup orange juice plus 2 Tbsp.
1 tsp. orange extract
1 tsp. grated orange peel (optional)
2½ cups flour
3 tsp. baking powder
¾ tsp. salt
¼ tsp. baking soda
½ tsp. cream of tartar

1) Set oven at 350 degrees.
2) Grease and flour tube pan. Sprinkle with pecans. Set aside.
3) In large mixing bowl, cream butter with electric mixer. Gradually add sugar, beating well. Add egg yolks one at a time, beating well.
4) In small bowl, combine orange juice, orange extract, and orange peel. Set aside.
5) In separate bowl, combine dry ingredients except cream of tartar. Then add dry

ingredients to creamed mixture alternating
with orange juice mixture.

6) In separate bowl, beat egg whites and cream of
   tartar until stiff peaks form. Fold into batter.
7) Pour into prepared pan. Bake at 350 for
   50–55 minutes. Cool in pan 10 minutes.
8) Remove from pan, punch holes in cake with
   a fork, and pour glaze (below) all over cake.

Glaze

½ tsp. grated orange peel
½ cup orange juice
¼ cup sugar
1 Tbsp. butter

1) While cake is cooling for 10 minutes in
   the pan, combine all glaze ingredients in
   saucepan and cook over medium heat,
   stirring constantly until sugar dissolves.
2) Pour over cake.
3) Enjoy! Yum, yum!

**Kristy Dykes** lives in sunny Florida with her husband, Milton, a minister. An award-winning author and former newspaper columnist, she's had hundreds of articles published in many publications, including two *New York Times* subsidiaries, *Guideposts Angels*, etc. She's written novellas in three other Barbour anthologies. Kristy is a public speaker, and one of her favorite topics is "How to Love Your Husband," based on Titus 2:4. Her goal in writing and speaking is to "put a smile on your face, a tear in your eye, and a glow in your heart." Fun fact: Kristy is a native Floridian, as are generations of her forebears (blow on fingertips, rub on shoulder). She loves hearing from her readers. Write her at kristydykes@aol.com or c/o Author Relations—Barbour Publishing, P.O. Box 719, Uhrichsville, OH 44683.

# MUSTANGS AND MISTLETOE

*by Pamela Griffin*

# Dedication

A special thank you to my helpful "critters"
Tamela H. M., Paige W. D., Lisa H., Lena D., Anne G.,
Mary H., Candice S., Molly N. B., and my mom.
And to my patient Lord—
even when life takes me on adventures
I may not ask for,
His plan is always for my good.

*"For I know the plans I have for you,"*
*declares the LORD, "plans to prosper you*
*and not to harm you,*
*plans to give you hope and a future."*
JEREMIAH 29:11

# Chapter 1

"Just exactly what kind of favor do you want from me?" Taylor Summerall hooked her hands on her hips and narrowly eyed her three brothers. Towering over her by a foot, Will and Robert stood to the side, clearly interested bystanders. Their oldest brother, Chad, leaned his forearm against the black banister near the bottom stair, putting him closer to a level with her modest height. He had that annoying, crooked smile on his face. The one Taylor always saw before he dropped the proverbial bomb.

Taylor tapped her satin pump against the parquet floor of the bed and breakfast's lobby. "I have a wedding to go to, and I have to be there, ready to walk down the aisle in half an hour. So you'd better make this snappy."

"Remember this past summer, when you wanted me

to take that friend of yours sightseeing?" Chad asked, a speculative gleam in his eye. "The one visiting from Colorado?"

"Sandy—yeah. So what? It turned out well for you. You both hit it off."

"But a deal was involved. Before I agreed to take her, you said you'd do anything I wanted. That you owed me one."

Taylor gave an impatient nod. What was this leading up to? Did he want her to wash his dirty laundry for a month? Clean his room? Do his chores? No, that was too juvenile and something he'd only made her do when they were both in high school.

"I have a friend from college who's coming to stay here through Christmas," Chad drawled. "He's an unmarried accountant from Chicago and will need someone to show him the ropes. Get him acquainted with ranch life—riding horseback, roping a calf, the whole nine yards. Show him around the place. Give him a good old Texas-sized welcome."

Unease crept up Taylor's spine. "Oh, no. No way, Chad. You do it."

He straightened from the staircase rail. "You owe me one. Remember?"

"He's right, Taylor," nineteen-year-old Will chimed in. "I'll be too busy helping Dad with chores needing done around the ranch, and Robert here has to study for finals. So we can't do it, either."

Robert nodded in silent assent, backing up both his older brothers.

Taylor bit back a groan. Why couldn't God have blessed her mother with all girls? Surely, three sisters wouldn't have been so demanding.

As though reading her mind, Chad softened. "I'm not asking you to marry the guy, Taylor. Only to do what you'd do for any other guest staying at the B and B. He'll be here longer than most since he's a buddy of mine."

"How long?" Taylor asked, frowning.

"Ten days—through Christmas, like I said. His mother just remarried and is on a cruise somewhere with her husband, so he doesn't have anywhere else to go for the holidays."

Wedding! At the reminder, Taylor glanced at the black wrought iron clock on the stucco wall. "I have to leave right now if I'm going to make it to church in time. Hailey will never forgive me if I hold things up and she's not married on the dot of three."

"And what about Derrick?" Chad insisted.

Taylor grabbed her matching rose-satin evening bag from a nearby chair. She threw the gold chain strap over her shoulder. "Could we please talk about this some other time?"

"Not really. He's coming tonight."

"Tonight!" Taylor hadn't checked the reservations list yet this week. The days preceding Christmas usually didn't bring a lot of people to The Silver Spur Ranch. "Oh, okay, fine. Whatever. Just a word of warning, Chad. Do *not* try to pair us off together. I'm perfectly satisfied with my life just the way it is."

Whirling around, she headed out the door and into a blast of Texas sunshine, though the wind from the north chilled her. Thinking of Kevin, the man to whom she once was engaged, tears skimmed her eyes. She fumbled for her keys and headed to her car.

❦

Twilight clouded the acres of grassy land and the woods beyond with dusky purple as Derrick Freeborn paid the driver, stepped out of the taxi, and grabbed his one suitcase.

So this was The Silver Spur.

To his right, a life-sized nativity scene sat on the ground, illuminated with white spotlights. The drive was lit up with red luminaries, giving the appearance of candles in small paper sacks, though when he moved closer to inspect one, he saw a glowing bulb inside. Again he looked up at the three-story ranch house, a relic of a bygone era. Dimly lit red, blue, and white strings of lights curled in a spiral around each of the five white columns at the front and echoed over the straight balcony rail above. Below that, a circular stained glass window featured the double S at a slant—the bottom curve of the first S tucked into the top curve of the second. Massive double doors stood between him and what would be home for the next ten days. On either side, an electric-lit cowboy boot in green kicked up its heel in welcome. Above, a red-lit sign declared, "Merry Christmas, Y'all!"

Derrick felt as if he were in alien country. He'd never been south of Chicago and wasn't sure why he'd accepted Chad's invitation to spend Christmas with his family. He certainly was no cowboy.

One thing astonished him—no oil wells. He'd harbored a rather silly boyhood belief that everyone from Texas must have a geyser in their backyard, even a capped or defunct one. The weather was colder than he expected it would be, too. Not bitterly cold and windy like Chicago, but cold enough for his suede jacket with its sheep's wool collar.

Well, come good or bad, he was here now. And, according to his recent doctor's visit, in crucial need of rest and relaxation, though how much of that he'd get on a ranch B and B was debatable. The small business firm for which he was a new accountant was going under, and he'd spent many a night examining the records kept in computer files. When he found evidence of possible embezzlement, he'd alerted his boss. Now an investigation was under way, and everyone's job was on the line.

Derrick headed up the four stairs of the cement porch and went inside, assuming that since the gargantuan ranch house was open to the public he should just go on in and not look for a doorbell. From somewhere, instrumental Christmas music was playing "Silent Night" featuring acoustical guitars. He nodded in approval as he took inventory of the empty lobby. Black and white tile floor. Western décor on the walls and shelves of a ceiling-high cabinet next to what appeared to be a receiving desk. Furniture—Spanish-Colonial-looking. A black wrought iron railing wound along the stairway, which was placed in an unusual jerky curve, as if the stair-layer had had the hiccups when he built them. Ten white stairs with a black-and-white-swirled runner made a gradual slope upward then stopped. A set of three more stairs catty-cornered from that, stopped, and a level ledge went for about five feet. Then a set of six stairs went up and stopped, angling off to another set of stairs. . . .

The sound of the door opening behind him and a breath of cold wind chilling his neck cut short his perusal. He turned to see a vision in a pink strapless gown. Hair the color of cinnamon lay in soft curls atop her head. Eyes, so light blue they almost appeared without color, drew him in. Her cheeks were chapped pink from the outside cold. She held a large bunch of red and white roses in one hand, but with both hands she pulled the ends of her fuzzy shawl up to her neck and tightly around her bare shoulders, as if hoping to hide her slim form in the shiny dress. She didn't break eye contact, though her expression was one of unease.

Derrick blurted the first thing that came to mind, "No one's here to check us in right now. I was just counting the stairs." He winced at his foolish statement.

Her eyebrows lifted. "Counting the stairs?"

"An odd habit of mine. Counting things. I like numbers."

"Oh." Her expression settled into disfavor. "You must be the accountant Chad told me about."

"Yes. I'm Derrick Freeborn." He walked the few paces between them and held out his hand. She gave it a reluctant halfhearted shake, then moved her arm to clutch her shawl tightly around herself again. Did she think he was going to jump her?

"How do you know Chad?" he asked.

"I'm his sister."

"Then you must be Taylor! I've heard a lot about you."

She pulled in her lips, as though exasperated. A faint dimple appeared in her left cheek. "I'll just see where Mother is. She's usually the one behind the desk."

Before he could answer, she was gone, her shoes rapidly clicking across the floor as she moved toward an opening on the left. No door blocked it and, curious, he moved to look into the next room. From his vantage point he could see a cozy fireplace, with the flames crackling inside, a mantel above it decorated with eight holiday knickknacks, and what must be a ten-foot Christmas tree nearby. A live one, if he could go by the smell of pine.

Suddenly she was back, the frown still on her face, the flowers missing. "Mother told me to tell you that she was sorry she wasn't here when you arrived. She had to take care of something that came up. I'll check you in."

He followed her back into the lobby, and she slipped around the waist-high counter, sitting down before a computer. She typed something on the keys, then stood and shoved a gold-embossed, red leather-bound book his way. "Please sign this. We like to keep a record of all our guests."

Her manner was polite but stiff, and Derrick sensed she'd rather be anywhere but with him. Once he set down the pen, she handed him a key with a plastic disk and the number 204.

"How many rooms do you have here?" he asked.

"Ten for the guests, not counting the private family rooms in another wing. You have the Lone Cowboy Room." She smiled, though it didn't reach her eyes. "Second door on the left at the end of the stairs. Enjoy your stay."

"Thanks." Picking up his one suitcase, he moved to

go, then snapped his fingers and turned to face her again. "One more thing. Chad mentioned something about the B and B offering lessons in horseback riding and other ranch-style activities?"

She visibly stiffened. "Yes. Though it's not mandatory. If you'd rather just stay in your room during your time here, that's fine, too."

Derrick hid a smile at her obvious effort to get rid of him. He didn't need two guesses as to who his teacher might be. "As long as I'm here, I'd like to give it a whirl. I've always wanted to learn how to ride a horse and rope a calf."

"Great," she said in a flat voice. "Your lesson will take place at seven-thirty—in the morning—so you'll need to eat breakfast early. In other words, no sleeping late."

"I think I can manage that. How many others are taking the course?"

She dropped her gaze to the open book. "Um, actually, it's just you."

This time he couldn't shield his grin. "Then I guess I'll be seeing you bright and early tomorrow morning, Teacher."

❦

Taylor watched Derrick climb the stairs. So, he'd figured out that she would be teaching him. Or had Chad relayed that information?

For a Chicago accountant, Derrick looked different than she'd imagined. She had pictured a meticulously neat, skinny man with a buzz haircut, pen sticking out of a shirt pocket, and wire-frame glasses. But that didn't describe the tall, strapping man taking the stairs. His dark hair grew a little long and fell in an easygoing wave over his forehead. His physique, under the casual, patterned block sweater and brown slacks, looked as if it was accustomed to regular workouts, and his mink-colored eyes yielded a wide range of emotions. From curious, to amused, to gentle. . .

At the stairs' ledge, he turned—and caught her staring up at him. He smiled and used one hand to lean against the banister.

"One last thing. When you see Chad, could you tell him I'm here? I'll be in my room if he wants to come up or phone me."

"Sure, I'll tell him." Taylor began busying herself with closing the guest book and replacing it and the pen on the counter beside the computer. She jotted a note to Chad and put it where he was sure to see it. When she felt it was safe, she looked up. Relief swept through her to find that the new guest had gone.

Taylor grabbed her purse and headed straight for her room to shimmy out of the embarrassing dress. Of all the outfits for Chad's friend to see her in! Hailey had insisted on strapless gowns for her bridesmaids, sure when she'd ordered them that the weather would cooperate. It hadn't. And though the neckline was modest compared to some of today's fashions, Taylor still thought it too low. Despite the heated banquet room and large crowd, she'd kept her mother's shawl tied around her shoulders throughout the reception, ignoring the smirks and lifted brows from the five other bridesmaids. Worse, though she'd tried to avoid it, she somehow had been the one to catch the bridal bouquet. Immediately she'd tossed it in another direction, as though she were playing Hot Potato. But her ploy hadn't worked, and she'd ended up with the roses. Then had come the teasing remarks about how "Mr. Right must be waiting just around the corner," the mild jokes, and the light but probing questions inquiring if there really was anyone in the wings.

Taylor let herself into her room, closed the door, and removed the offensive dress, pulling it over a hanger. She slid into her comfortable, toasty warm flannel pajamas and breathed a sigh of relief. Grabbing her Bible, she settled into bed, pulling the petal-soft sheets and thick quilt around her, and prepared to spend a few minutes soaking up God's Word. She was almost to the end of the chapter before she was cut short by the shrill ring of her bedside phone. Seeing it was an inside call by the blinking button, she nabbed the receiver.

"Yes?"

"You sent him to bed without supper?" Chad's question came back. "At six o'clock in the evening?"

She rolled her eyes toward the ceiling. "And how was I supposed to know he hadn't already eaten?" She squirmed, feeling a tinge of remorse when she remembered her cool treatment toward the new guest and her objective to rid herself of his presence quickly. "He could've said something if he was hungry."

"True, but to my knowledge most B and Bs don't offer dinner, so he probably didn't know he was invited. He's my guest, Taylor, and he's spending time with our family—that means all the meals and private parties. Get used to it. And telling him he had to eat breakfast before seven-thirty or he couldn't have his riding lesson was pretty lame, too."

Taylor muttered something not fit to be aired, then silently repented. "I didn't say it like that. Is that what he told you?"

"He didn't tell me anything. But when I rang his room to invite him to dinner and he said that he had to get to bed early or he'd miss his riding lesson, I figured you were up to something."

"I am. I have to help Mom plan for this Friday. The Graystones are coming for their annual visit and are renewing their wedding vows—it's their fiftieth anniversary.

A morning lesson works best for me."

"Yeah, but seven-thirty? Since when do you give lessons that early? Most guests like to sleep in their first night here. And they don't go to bed hungry."

Taylor frowned. "If you're so concerned about his eating and sleeping habits, then why didn't *you* stick around to check him in?"

"I had to run to the store. Anyway, Mom wants to know if you're coming down to eat."

She sank back against her pillow. "No. I ate plenty at the wedding reception. I think I'll just go to bed early. I have a busy morning ahead teaching your college chum how to play cowboy." She couldn't keep the bite out of her words. How had she ever let him rope her into such a situation?

There was an uncomfortable pause. "Listen, Taylor, I'm sorry if I came across heavy-handed this afternoon and pushed you into this. It's just that when I was in Chicago, Derrick showed me a really good time, and I want to return the favor."

"Okay, so remind me again why you're not the one hanging out with him and I'm stuck with the job?"

"Besides my usual chores, I've got other things around the ranch that I need to help Dad with. Things that won't wait 'til after Christmas."

Taylor understood, though she didn't have to like it.

She was generally the one who taught the guests to ride. She and her younger two brothers, and they had their own convenient excuses.

"Anyhow, I'm sorry," Chad said again.

"You're forgiven." Taylor was accustomed to her brother's phone apologies. He didn't like face-to-face meetings that involved an admission of guilt on his part, and since all the phones in the ranch house were connected to the main desk, including the family's bedroom phones, Chad had developed this method of communicating when he wanted forgiveness.

"See you in the morning."

"Yeah, good night." Taylor replaced the phone and stared at it.

Ten days. Hopefully the time would fly past and the Yankee from the Windy City would blow back to his Chicago home, and then everything would be on an even kilter again. She supposed ten days wasn't so bad. After all, what was ten days?

She remembered what Derrick said about liking to count things, and her mind took up the challenge. *Let's see, that was one week, three days. . .two hundred and forty hours. . .fourteen thousand and four hundred minutes. . .*

With Derrick joining in on all the family doings.

She punched her pillow, then turned off the light and threw herself down on her side. What kind of person liked to count things, anyway? It reminded her of that silly purple puppet on *Sesame Street*. And why was she dwelling on this? He was just another guest, after all. Most guests stayed two or three or even four days, so ten wasn't all that much more.

After long minutes of staring into darkness, Taylor realized she'd forgotten to brush her teeth. Grumbling, she flicked on the light again and headed for her private bathroom.

*Eight hundred and sixty-four thousand seconds.*

Ten days was really an eternity.

# Chapter 2

With a satisfied smile, Derrick strode toward the stables after a filling breakfast. He'd never had hot salsa on scrambled eggs before—and over steak, yet—but the combination wasn't half bad. And he'd never considered pinto beans to be a breakfast dish, but the helping he'd eaten was actually tasty. A frosty chill lingered in the air though the sun was out, and he could see his breath form a white fog, even smell the trace of jalapeño peppers as he exhaled. The spicy meal had warmed his blood and set his motor running. He was ready for anything—be it a fidgety horse or a prickly female.

The female stepped outside the dim stables, leading a dark gray horse. With the reins in one hand, she settled her fists on her jean-clad hips. "You're late."

Derrick held up his hands in mock defense. "Not my fault. Chad wanted to talk to me about something. I promise to be on time tomorrow."

"Humph." Taylor's gaze slid down his form, and she arched a brow. "Let me guess. You bought that outfit just for this week."

"Is there something wrong with it?" Derrick looked down at his black designer jeans and cream-colored Western shirt with the red braid. They matched the red cowboy boots he'd found on clearance, and the black felt hat went nicely with the outfit.

Her mouth flickered at the corners. "As long as the jeans are tough and the boots are durable, it'll work, I guess." She dipped her head and pulled down the brim of her tan cowboy hat as she turned toward the horse, as though to hide the amusement he detected in her eyes. He noticed that beneath her brown suede jacket her plaid shirt and jeans weren't flashy, but looked worn and comfortable. As did her brown leather boots.

"Today we'll just go over the basics," Taylor said. "Mounting, dismounting, learning the commands, getting a feel for the saddle and how to use the reins. I've already saddled Thunder, so I'll show you how to do that tomorrow."

"Thunder?" Derrick darted an uncertain look toward the gray beast.

Taylor smiled. "Not to worry. Thunder really should have been called *Breeze*. He's a good old boy, aren't you?" She affectionately stroked the white blaze along the horse's forehead.

He tossed his head as if nodding, and she smiled. Derrick liked her smile when it was real. Not fake or mocking or tight. Just nice and easy, a sweet spread of her lips that put a sparkle in her eyes. Last night when he'd met her, she'd been wearing light makeup on her eyelids, cheeks, and lips, and her hair was done up in curls pinned on top of her head. Today her face was scrubbed fresh, and he spotted a sprinkling of freckles on her nose and cheeks. Her thick hair was pulled back in one long ponytail that brushed her shoulder blades. He preferred this look to the glamorous one of yesterday. It fit her better.

She glanced in his direction and frowned. "What are you smiling at?"

"Nothing." He sensed it was smarter to keep his thoughts to himself.

Her narrowed eyes continued to survey him. "All right, then. Let's get started. First, put your left boot in the stirrup and your left hand on the saddle. Then hoist yourself up and throw your right leg over the horse. I'll hold the reins and keep the horse steady."

"Yes, ma'am," he said in his best Texas drawl as he tipped his hat. "Anything to please."

He settled his heel against the stirrup and followed the rest of her directions, but his right leg wouldn't cooperate. The new jeans were stiff and tight and he couldn't swing his leg all the way over. If he tried, he might rip the seam.

"Is there a problem?" she asked when he tried a second time and remained precariously perched, one boot in the stirrup, both arms clutched across the smooth cowhide saddle, and his right leg raised like a dog at a hydrant. The horse nickered and moved its head as though trying to look back to see what kind of idiot he was paired with.

"Uh, no," Derrick grunted. "Almost have it now." Instead of trying to move his leg higher, he shifted his upper body by giving a little jump to hoist himself over. The slick sole of his boot slipped off the metal stirrup, his chin hit the saddle, and he landed in the dust at Taylor's feet.

He looked up. Her head was lowered as she rubbed the middle of her forehead with three fingers. He brushed his hand along the underside of his chin to check for blood. Seeing none, he shrugged.

"Maybe I can get a refund on the outfit."

At this, she let out a laughing snort, as if she couldn't hold back any longer. He liked the sound of it and grinned. She lifted her head and met his gaze, her smile as wide as his, then she shook her head as though exasperated.

"Are you all right?"

"Sure. I'm tough."

"Okay, then. Go ask my mother to loan you a pair of Will's jeans. You look like you wear the same size. I'll wait for you here."

Derrick picked up his hat from the ground where it had fallen and managed to climb to his feet, though awkwardly, as the stiff denim pressed hard into his skin. Maybe he shouldn't have washed the jeans before wearing them or dried them on high heat. He'd worn jeans before, of course, but yesterday morning he'd done a rush packing job and had put all the new clothes on a fast dry cycle. Obviously a big mistake. At least the shirt had survived.

He headed toward the main house, embarrassed, but glad he'd been the one to make Taylor laugh. According to Chad, she didn't do much of that anymore.

❧

Sunlight poured over the tall man in the saddle as Taylor watched him guide Thunder in a circle around the stable yard. The Yank caught on quick, she'd give him that. Once he returned wearing a pair of smooth, faded blue jeans—ones that didn't look as if they would cut off his circulation if he sneezed—he'd succeeded in mounting the horse. A bit awkwardly, but he'd gotten up there.

"Chad-tells-me-this-is-a-working-ranch," Derrick said, his words bouncing up and down with his body as the horse started at a trot.

Taylor grinned at how funny he sounded, even if she was exasperated that his questions seemed to increase with the horse's speed. She'd never known a man who liked to talk much, but this one did. "The cowhands work on another part of the ranch, away from the B and B. The only time you'll see any of them up close and personal is when one of them, probably Buddy, will show you how to rope a cow."

"You-won't-be-doing-that?"

"Nope. That goes beyond my level of expertise." Unease pricked her. Hopefully he would be satisfied with her answer and not pry.

"How-big-is-this-ranch?"

"Over two thousand acres. My great-grandfather trained mustangs here, but now we raise beef cattle." She stood in the middle of the corral, turning in slow circles as she watched his progress. "Since you're so interested in the life of a cowboy, I guess you should've come to the B and B earlier. We had a five-day cattle drive several weeks ago. Two of our guests went with Chad, my father, and the cowhands to experience a real Wild West adventure."

"Sorry-to-have-missed-it," Derrick said in staccato bursts. "But-Chad-told-me-about-the-Saturday-night-campout. He-said-you're-in-charge-of-that."

Taylor stiffened in irritated surprise. So she'd been

volunteered to host another function without her knowledge? Did her brothers think she had nothing else to do?

Derrick glanced her way. "I'm-looking-forward-to-it."

Peeved, for a wild moment Taylor thought about slapping Thunder's rump and sending the horse into a fast gallop that would take its talkative rider far from her. Maybe then Derrick would lose interest in future lessons. Of course she wouldn't endanger any guest's life by doing something as crazy as that, but the delectable thought still made her grin.

Derrick rode the horse in another full circle. A dog's rapid barking suddenly yipped through the air, seizing Taylor's attention. A brown flash of fur zipped past Thunder, followed by a black one. The horse spooked, whinnying in fright, then took off like a shot out of the stable yard. Taylor groaned when she saw that someone had left the gate open.

"Hold on!" she called to Derrick.

His face tensed as he clutched the reins and pommel in a white-knuckled grip, doing his best to stay astride the horse as it cleared the gate. Taylor mounted her mustang saddled nearby. She prodded the white-spotted gelding into a hard run, soon catching up to Thunder, who was over a mile away from the stable. Thankfully, the city boy hadn't fallen. He was draped over the horse, his thighs squeezing the saddle.

"Pull on the reins to stop him," she called. "Don't squeeze your legs tight. That only makes him run faster."

"What?"

"Don't squeeze your legs!"

"Then how am I supposed to stay on?" he shouted incredulously.

"Unwrap your arms from around his neck, and pull on the reins."

Tight-lipped, Derrick straightened from his hunched-over position and followed her orders.

"Easy, Thunder," she commanded, reaching for the horse's reins and pulling on them harder. "Whoa, boy."

The horse slowed to a walk, then came to a standstill. Taylor reined in Stardust and looked over at Derrick. His hat was missing, and his face was stretched in an expression of pain. In fact, he looked a little green around the gills.

"Are you okay?" she asked.

"What happened?" Derrick's words sounded vague.

"Some dog was chasing a squirrel. I've never seen it around here before."

"The dog or the squirrel?" He groaned, pushing a hand to his stomach. "Never mind. That was some ride."

Her remorse deepened. "Sorry."

"It wasn't your fault."

Maybe not, but she still felt guilty. Hadn't she pictured the scenario of Thunder galloping off with Derrick only moments before it actually happened?

"Are you going to throw up?" she asked.

"I don't think so, but my stomach feels like it's still on a wild ride. Must be something I ate."

"I never thought jalapeños made great breakfast material, but my brother likes things hot and spicy. We do serve normal breakfasts here, too. Before our lesson tomorrow, I'll make you a ham and cheese omelet with hash browns and pumpkin-nut muffins—to make up for what happened just now," she added hastily when she saw his face relax and his eyes brighten. No use giving him the wrong idea.

"It sounds like something to look forward to. When I can think about food again."

"Good." She shifted in the saddle. "We should be getting back now. I'll show you how to unsaddle Thunder. Then your lesson will be over for today and you can go lie down if you want. Do you remember how to give the command for Thunder to walk?"

"Sure." He lifted the reins, leaned forward, and clicked his tongue against the roof of his mouth. Thunder began to move slowly forward in a straight line, in the opposite direction of the stables. "Uh, how do I get him to turn?" Derrick called over his shoulder when the horse carried him closer to a fringe of bare cottonwoods.

"Use the reins. Gently pull one rein to the side in the

direction you want Thunder to go."

She watched as Derrick got the horse under control and swung him around, then prodded Stardust to walk beside Thunder. She was uncomfortably aware of the casual glances Derrick cast her way, but she didn't look at him. She might feel guilty about the riding lesson and want to make up for it, but that was as far as her feelings went. He was Chad's friend and a temporary guest. Nothing more.

At the gate, a blond-haired woman and child waited. A black puppy fidgeted in the boy's arms. "I'm sorry," the woman said. "We couldn't find anyone to sit with Pepper, and he doesn't like kennels. The lady who owns the place said it would be okay if we brought him. As soon as we got out of the car, he jumped out and ran this way. I'm Rhea Graystone, and this is my son, Brandon."

"Pleased to meet you. I'm Taylor Summerall, and this is one of our guests, Derrick Freeborn," she said with a smile and a polite tip of her hat. "In the future, please keep your dog away from the stables. There's a fenced-in backyard where he can run. The horses don't know him and can get easily spooked, like what happened with Derrick just now."

Rhea's gaze went to Derrick, and she frowned. "Are you all right?"

"No real harm done," he said. "The ride was an

adventure, but I think I'd better get back to my room. If you don't mind, I'd rather learn how to unsaddle another day."

Concern pricked Taylor again. "We'll have a better lesson tomorrow." She gave him directions on how to dismount, slipping off her own horse first as an example. As she led both Stardust and Thunder to the stable, she watched Derrick limp to the main house. The Yank had gumption, a friendly personality—and he wasn't hard to look at, either.

Frowning, Taylor turned away and busied herself with unsaddling both horses.

❧

"Is there something about me your sister doesn't like?" Derrick asked Chad as he helped himself to a thick slice of pumpkin pie and cup of eggnog after the roast beef and potato dinner. The dessert table was set out in buffet, all-you-can-eat style, and Derrick was taking advantage of it. In the background of the cozy family room the stereo speakers played a silly Christmas country ditty, a song Derrick didn't recognize. Something about the singer's grandma getting run over by a reindeer.

"Interesting song," Derrick commented.

Chad chuckled. "Yeah, Dad likes to listen to the radio in the evenings for the local news. About Taylor. . ." He looked toward his sister, who stood across the room, her body language rigid as she stared into the tranquil fire. "She's like that with all the guys," Chad said. "She takes off running like a frightened calf being chased by a coyote if anyone gets too close."

Derrick mulled over the information while he let the rich, creamy eggnog slide over his tongue. "Why? Did she get hurt? She doesn't seem like the shy type."

Chad let out a loud guffaw. "Taylor—shy? Not my sister," he added more quietly when she turned and looked their way, her gaze sharp. A repentant look crossed his face. "Go easy on her, Derrick. She lost a fiancé two years ago and hasn't gotten over it yet."

"Two years is a long time to grieve over a broken relationship."

"Yeah, that's what we all think," Chad relented. "But it wasn't that kind of breakup. Kevin was killed in a freak accident, and Taylor was there when it happened."

Before Derrick could inquire further, Taylor began walking across the maroon-colored pile carpet toward them. "And what are you two old buddies chatting about?" she asked sweetly, the look in her eyes suspicious.

"Oh, just what two old friends usually wind up talking about," Chad shot back. "The past."

"Yeah, but whose?"

A hint of red seeped beneath Chad's skin. "I just remembered. Mom wants me to help move some furniture in the banquet room. I'll be back in a few." He weaseled away through the exit into the lobby.

"Chicken," Taylor muttered under her breath. She pinpointed Derrick with her pale blue eyes. The gemstone-blue sweater she wore brought out the narrow rim of darker blue around her stunning irises. "What about you? Are you brave enough to tell the truth?"

"We were talking about you," Derrick admitted, feeling a little sheepish.

"I gathered that when I heard Chad blurt my name. So what did he tell you?"

"Among other things, he told me you lost your fiancé in an accident."

Surprise jolted her expression, and a flash of pain tinged her eyes. "He shouldn't have done that."

"Maybe not. Anyway, I'm sorry."

Taylor shrugged and looked beyond him. She lifted her crystal cup and took a sip of eggnog.

"I lost someone close, too, once. My kid sister. I know it's not the same thing, but I just wanted you to know I understand."

She was quiet a moment before she sought his gaze. "How'd it happen?"

"She was in a carpool with a bunch of kids in a station wagon. Another car ran a red light and broadsided them. Jenny was sitting by the door and was the only one killed. She was eight at the time."

Her brows pulled down in a sympathetic frown. "That must have been hard."

"It was. I had a lot of guilt to deal with."

"Guilt?"

"I was sixteen and had just gotten my license. I was the one who was supposed to pick her up from school. But I ran into some friends and forgot." He cleared his throat. The words were still difficult to speak, though time had eased the pain and he'd already dealt with the guilt years ago through counseling.

Her expression softened. She laid her hand on the sleeve of the green turtleneck he'd thrown on before dinner. "I'm sorry," she said. "Believe me, I know how difficult that must have been."

Somehow the tables had turned. His initial reason for bringing up the subject was to get her to talk about losing Kevin; but now she was the one doling out sympathy. He wasn't even sure why he spoke about the experience with Jenny, unless it was to reassure Taylor that others dealt with similar tragedies and survived. He'd only known the woman twenty-four hours, but already he felt connected to her in some odd way.

Whether or not she would have spoken about what happened two years ago, Derrick would never know. At that moment, Taylor's mom glided up to them. "I'm so glad y'all could come and be with us this Christmas, Derrick," she enthused in a Southern drawl that would've sounded more at home in Georgia than Texas. Dressed in a shimmering white pantsuit flared at the legs and sleeves, the woman with the reddish-brown hair and pale blue eyes, much like Taylor's, was the picture of a charming hostess. "It's so nice to get to know one of Chad's friends."

"It's a pleasure to be here, Mrs. Summerall. Thanks for having me."

"Anytime. And please, call me Charla. Now where was it that Chad said your mother and her new husband went off to on their honeymoon?"

"They took a Caribbean cruise."

"Oh, yes, how lovely! It must be wonderful to get away from all that cold weather y'all have up North. Brrrr," she said with a little mock-rubbing of her arms. "Which reminds me, Taylor. I heard on the weather radio this morning that it may drop to the twenties Saturday night. Be sure to wear your thermals, and take the insulated sleeping bags."

Taylor's cheeks went pink. "Actually, maybe we should call off the campout if there's bad weather forecasted."

"Oh, no, the skies are supposed to be clear that night. And the Graystones—not the couple getting married, but their grandson and his wife—have expressed an interest in participating. They used to live in Michigan, so I'm sure they wouldn't mind the chilly temperature. And I'll bet Derrick, here, has seen his share of cold weather, too."

Derrick nodded, though he wasn't sure he wanted to sleep on the frozen ground if it was going to be all that cold.

As if reading his mind, Charla chuckled. "We have the latest in winter-weather camping gear, so don't you worry. We won't let you turn into an icicle."

Derrick let out a sound resembling a short laugh, though he still wasn't too sure. "You mentioned a wedding here this weekend?"

"The Graystones are celebrating their golden wedding anniversary," Taylor answered. "They'll be renewing their wedding vows."

"Which reminds me," Charla said. "I need to call Mabel and make sure she can play the piano for the reception. You're welcome to come, if you'd like, Derrick. The Graystones are a very sweet and outgoing couple. They've spent every anniversary with us since we opened four years ago. And Taylor is going to sing. Now you be sure to help yourself to those pumpkin cookies." She smiled at Derrick, then disappeared as quickly as she'd come.

"You're going to sing?"

Taylor went a shade redder. "I'm not that great or anything. I'm just free." She grinned self-consciously. "Don't feel obligated to come. The Graystones are the type who don't want anyone to feel left out, and they asked Mom to give a blanket invitation to any guests staying here. But you're the only one staying, besides the Graystones' family, of course."

"Actually, I'd like to come." When Charla first spoke of it, the thought of attending hadn't crossed Derrick's mind. Hearing that Taylor would sing raised his interest level by ten points. Saturday couldn't get here fast enough. Though if he were going to ride a horse to the campsite, as Chad had said he would have to do, he would need a lot more improvement. Tomorrow's riding lesson just had to go better. And hopefully his relationship with the teacher would improve, too.

# Chapter 3

"M om, I can't find the gold and crimson poinsettias." Taylor stood on a ladder and searched the high shelves of the storage closet, sorting through the stacks of thick plastic zippered cases that had once contained sheet sets or comforters. Now they were containers for silk flowers, arranged by theme and color for every occasion.

"Taylor, if it was a rattlesnake it would've bitten you," her mom said, exasperation starting to show through her usual poise. It was always like that the day before a big event took place. Mom often got high-strung, worried that this or that might go wrong. "Near your left elbow, under the blue orchids and white daisies."

"Oh." Taylor nabbed the light but bulky pillow-sized case from the stack, let it fall the several feet to the carpet, then stepped down from the ladder to reclaim it.

"White tablecloths with the gold lacy edging, or gold tablecloths with embroidered roses?"

Taylor worked to free the zipper on the case. It stuck, and she tugged harder. As she worked to loosen the metal teeth, she thought about her morning ride.

"Taylor! Did you hear me?"

Taylor looked up. "What? Oh, sorry, Mom. I was off in another world."

"One with Derrick in it?"

Taylor frowned. "Why would you say that?"

"Because since he arrived four days ago, you've acted differently."

"Differently?" Taylor shook her head. "No, I'm the same. I sure hope, though, that Mabel will be feeling well enough to play tomorrow. But if I have to sing a cappella, I guess I can manage." She steered the conversation to the wedding, sure that this was the appropriate path on which to sidetrack her mother. "Hopefully, I won't prove to be too much of a disappointment."

"You'll do fine, dear. You have a lovely voice. Now, which tablecloths do you think will work best?"

"The lacy ones." Taylor held the flower case to her chest. "I'll just go put these in some vases."

"Use the glass ones with the gold flecks. I think that would be a nice touch."

Taylor moved away before her mother could reintroduce their prior conversation. It annoyed her that the entire family seemed bent on hitching her with Derrick. Robert and Will, with their pathetically obvious efforts to make sure Taylor sat beside Derrick at dinner every night. Dad, with his never-ending questions regarding Derrick's job—at one point, Taylor wouldn't have been surprised if her father had asked to see Derrick's annual tax returns for the last two years. And good old Chad, who'd lassoed her into giving Derrick riding lessons and taking him on the campout tomorrow night. At least her older brother had taken over the calf-roping lesson, since Buddy wasn't available. Taylor wasn't sure she could've handled that.

Regardless, this morning, curiosity had compelled her to peek inside the building that housed the life-sized mechanical horse and calf. Derrick had sat atop the horse, his profile to her. Some wisenheimer had fastened a red velvet Santa hat to the fiberglass calf, which whizzed away from the stationary horse on a fifteen-foot track, making it harder for the rider to lasso it. Taylor wondered why Chad had turned the ride to expert level, then realized Derrick probably wouldn't have been happy with trying to rope a stationary calf. His first awkward attempts brought loud guffaws from both men, and Taylor grinned. That's one thing that amazed Taylor about Derrick. He had the ability to laugh at himself and get others laughing with him, not at him. Also, he was persistent. After four days of riding lessons, he was getting better. He'd taken a hard fall or two to reach that mark, though she'd tried to show him the proper way to relax and take a fall. He might have had the trim, muscular build of a cowboy, but he was as clumsy as a gangly junior high kid.

As Taylor stood in the banquet room and arranged metallic gold roses and poinsettias with the deep crimson ones, adding silk greenery as needed, Derrick's disappointed words from that morning came back to haunt her. "But don't I get to rope a real calf?" he'd asked Chad when the lesson was over.

Then as now, Taylor felt an awkward lump clog her throat, bringing with it the sting of tears. At the barn, she'd lifted her hand to swipe them away, painfully knocking her elbow against the door, alerting both men to her presence. Chad's expression turned sympathetic as realization hit, and he opened his mouth to speak. But she shook her head and backed up, then turned and hurried home, her fast walk soon speeding into a run as memories took hold and tears dribbled down her cheeks.

The bitter image of two years ago soured the sweet silliness of Derrick's morning lesson, and she swallowed the emotion down hard. She would not cry again. Viciously, she jammed a piece of greenery deep into a vase.

"Ouch!" an amused male voice said from behind her. "I hope that wasn't aimed at me for being such a lousy student this week."

Startled, she spun around. The smile on Derrick's face faded to worry. "Hey, are you crying?" He spanned the ten-foot distance between them.

"I'm fine." Briskly she wiped under her eyes with the back of her free hand and lifted her chin, hoping to give the impression of being in control. "You shouldn't sneak up on people like that."

"Sorry. Carpet muffles sound." He looked around the formal banquet room in the throes of being decorated. "Anything I can do to help?"

"You're a guest."

"Yeah, but you guys have made me feel like part of your family. I'd like to contribute something."

Taylor shrugged. "You can set up the folding tables and chairs. They're in the closet, outside the door. We'll need six tables. The guests will sit in the center of the room, and the guests of honor will sit at the dining room table that Chad moved against the wall over there."

Derrick went to retrieve the items. Taylor tried to concentrate on the flower arrangements, but the constant clanging as Derrick set up the metal furniture, and dropped a chair in the process, drew her attention his way. She watched the muscles in his back and shoulders bunch and ripple under the thin maroon pullover as he went about his task. The ends of dark hair brushing the lower edge of his collar curled like shining, mocha gift ribbons. They were clumped together and damp, as if he'd just gotten out of a shower.

"Must you make so much noise?" she bit out.

Still in his hunched-over position, he looked over his shoulder in surprise. "Sorry. The table leg was stuck, and I was trying to bang it into place."

Instant remorse hit. "No, I'm sorry. I shouldn't have snapped." She massaged her right temple with the fingertips of one hand. "You were nice to offer to help, and I'm acting like a shrew."

"Headache?"

She nodded. "I'm pretty well finished with these. Could you tell Mom I went to lie down for a while?"

"Sure." He straightened and faced her. "I hope you feel better soon."

"Thanks." Taylor left the room and went upstairs. Why did the guy have to be so nice? It would be easier to be indifferent toward him if he weren't so helpful and kind. And the way her stomach quivered when he looked at her with those velvety brown eyes didn't help matters, either. What was happening to her?

❦

Awed, Derrick watched Taylor the following morning.

She stood at the front of the gaily decorated banquet room, clothed in a mellow white floor-length gown rimmed in lace. Something shiny sparkled all over her hair, like silvery moondust. Her hair was anchored on top of her head in a waterfall of curls, as it had been the first time he'd met her.

She was beautiful.

Derrick found it hard to catch his breath as he listened to her sing with the voice of an angel, which she resembled. No background music marred the pure, sweet notes as she sang to the golden wedding couple a song Taylor had told him was played on their original wedding day, "Oh, Promise Me."

Tears glistened in both Mr. Graystone's and his wife's eyes as Taylor finished the last hauntingly sweet verse. Afterward, the white-haired gentleman turned to the smiling woman he had lived beside for half of a century and tenderly kissed her. Once they broke apart, the guests clapped and cheered, and corks of champagne were popped.

"To another fifty years, as great as the first," Mr. Graystone's son called out, lifting his glass.

"Hear, hear!" The elderly gentleman laughed, giving his plump wife a squeeze.

Derrick watched Taylor, who mixed with the guests, accepting their praise and serving white-frosted lemon cake to whoever wanted it. Though she was outgoing, Derrick could see how stiffly she carried herself. It was some time before he could get her alone.

"You sing beautifully," he said.

"Thank you." Her face and smile looked as rigid as porcelain, and just as ready to crack. "I wish we would've had piano music to go with it, though."

She started to move away, and Derrick grappled for words to keep her with him. "Are we still on for tonight?"

"The weather situation hasn't changed, if that's what you mean."

"I can handle the cold."

"Then I guess we're on. I'll see you at the stable at five."

"Taylor?"

She turned, her brows lifted.

"Is anything wrong? You don't act as if you're feeling well. Is the headache back?"

The stiffly polite look diminished, and a trace of genuine warmth touched her pale blue eyes. "I'm okay. Thanks for asking. Weddings are just sometimes difficult for me."

"Because of Kevin?" he asked softly.

"Partly."

She attempted a smile, one that trembled at the corners. Derrick suddenly had a strong urge to kiss that smile into full bloom but took a swig of his sherbet-covered punch instead.

"I'd better go prepare for tonight," she said. "The campout is only a few hours away."

For Derrick, those hours crawled by. He'd already packed his gear that morning, so he spent the time at his windows, watching Taylor and her brothers entering and exiting one of the ranch buildings as they geared up for the night ahead. He would have gone down to help, but he sensed that Taylor needed some distance, to sort things out. That he was getting to her was obvious, and he wasn't sure how that made him feel. Could she ever think about him the way he was starting to think about her?

At five before five, Derrick hoisted his backpack from the wide brown leather saddle used to decorate the dark-paneled corner of the room. He plucked his hat from the two-foot-high bronze cowboy statue on the oak dresser, slapped it on his head, and headed for the stable.

The horses for the young Graystones and their two small sons were already saddled, and Taylor was making adjustments to one of the horse's stirrups. She looked up as he approached. "Ready?"

"I sure am." Under her supervision, he saddled Thunder. When she didn't have to correct him once, as had been the case before, he grinned. "Did I pass, Teacher?"

She smiled. "With flying colors. But now comes the real test."

Derrick curbed his anxiety. He'd never been on an hour-long trail ride. Or an overnight campout. Would he prove to be too much of a city boy to handle it? During his last visit, the doctor had told him he needed to take it easy, that his life was too stressful, especially with the new job, and at the rate he kept it up, he'd have a heart attack before hitting thirty. Derrick wouldn't call the past four days of learning to ride, being captive on a runaway horse, and learning how to rope a calf easy, but he'd had fun. And he'd never felt better a day in his life. Thinking about work, Derrick frowned. Chicago, with its steel and glass skyscrapers and congested traffic, seemed a world away.

Riding Thunder, who plodded behind Stardust along a grassy hill, Derrick inhaled a deep breath of chilly air. Sunset painted the far-reaching sky with splashes of red, purple, and gold. Acres of wheat-colored grass shifted slightly in the breeze, and short, squat trees lined the snakelike stream to his right. A herd of white-faced brown cattle grazed nearby. A cowboy rode between them, probably counting them, as Chad had said they needed to do each day. For grins, Derrick took up the challenge from his place on the hill.

Taylor reined in her horse, waiting for Derrick to catch up.

"Doing all right?" she asked.

He smiled. "Just counting the cows."

She grinned, then laughed. "I had to ask! Anyway, I wanted to let you know that we should reach camp before dark. Will and Robert went there earlier to set up for us."

"I was wondering where the tents were."

"Since we were getting such a late start because of the golden wedding, I asked my brothers to set them up in advance."

"It was a nice ceremony. I don't usually go to that sort of thing, but I was glad to be there."

"Yeah, it was nice." Taylor's gaze grew introspective. "It's nice to know that two people who've lived together so long can still love one another so much."

"It takes a lot of love to make a marriage work," Derrick agreed. "And commitment. You have to want the same things."

Taylor threw him a sharp glance, then looked away. "Yeah. I need to check on the others." Her expression now grim, she headed a few yards back down the trail to where the Graystone bunch rode.

Derrick wondered what he'd said to reap her curt words.

❦

Taylor stared into the sizzling, crackling campfire. Wrapped in several layers of clothes and sitting close to the moderate blaze, she felt toasty warm on the outside. But inside, her heart was a lump of ice.

165

She watched Derrick joke with the two Graystone boys as he squished a fat marshmallow on a pointed stick and held it in the middle of the flames. It caught fire, and he quickly withdrew it and blew the flame out. "That's okay," he said with a smile. "I like mine cinder-black."

Taylor blew out a breath in amused exasperation. "Don't you know how to do anything, city boy?" She impaled a marshmallow on a stick and held it over the tip of the flames, rotating it until the white, puffy square turned a delicious golden-brown. Taking it from the fire, she trapped it between two graham crackers and a section of a semisweet chocolate bar then offered it his way. "Here."

Instead of taking the s'mores, which she held near his face, Derrick opened his mouth for the treat. She hesitated, heart beating fast, then crammed the thing halfway into his mouth, withdrawing her hand as quickly as she could.

"Thanks," he said, mouth full. He brushed away the downpour of crumbs that had fallen to his jacket as a result of her hasty gesture. His eyes were laughing at her, and she quickly looked away to make her own snack.

"Let's sing Christmas carols!" eleven-year-old Brandon Graystone suggested. "I brought my harmonica."

Taylor grinned. "I'll get my guitar."

"You play guitar, too?" Derrick asked.

"Yep, though I'd reserve any praise until you hear me. I'm not that good."

"That's what you led me to believe about your singing."

Taylor pretended not to hear Derrick's words. She walked past the blanketed horses tied near the fire and toward her tent to claim the guitar case her brothers had brought earlier in the pickup, along with the rest of the bulky gear. A camp stove nearby held a hot pot of coffee, and she refilled her tin mug before going back to the circle. The stove was used to heat the dinner stew, the coffee, and the hot water for cocoa for the kids—but it couldn't toast marshmallows. For that, a campfire was needed. Besides, singing around a stove didn't produce half the fun singing around a campfire did. And the guests expected it.

After Taylor reclaimed her spot next to Derrick and tuned her guitar, she strummed out a Texas-style version of "Deck the Halls." Brandon joined in with his harmonica, if not expertly, then exuberantly. But his playing didn't sound any worse than Taylor's. She ignored the chords struck wrong and belted out a round of carols, giving them a Western twang, with everybody merrily joining in and having a rollicking good time.

After awhile, the songs grew more mellow, more worshipful, and the others stopped singing, instead listening to Taylor. Her eyes half closed, a smile on her face, she strummed her guitar and sang her two favorites: "The Holly and the Ivy" and "What Child Is This?" Then she ended with the slow and peaceful "Silent Night." With the stars twinkling above, and not even a breeze to stir the few leaves left on the nearby cottonwoods, the song seemed fitting.

"That was beautiful," Rhea Graystone said softly. "I can't remember having such a good time."

"Me, either!" Brandon said. "Can we do it again tomorrow?"

They all laughed, and Derrick mussed the boy's hair. Brandon giggled. Derrick then jabbed the boy's side in a tickle, and Brandon squealed, laughing louder. His eight-year-old brother, Joshua, obviously not wanting to be left out, jumped up behind Derrick and, growling like a bear, pretended to put him in a choke hold. Derrick reached behind with both hands and tickled him.

"Not so close to the fire, guys," Taylor warned softly.

Derrick was so good with kids. He would make a great father someday. Kevin never wanted them, though he'd told Taylor that after they were married five years and settled into their life together, maybe he'd give in to her desire for children and think about having one then. Again Taylor thought about Derrick's words on the ride out here, of how a good marriage was based on commitment and wanting the same things.

"It's your bedtime," Mr. Graystone said. "Say good night to everyone."

"Aw, do we have to, Dad?" Joshua asked.

"I'm fixing to hit my bedroll, too," Derrick said.

"Fixing?" Brandon giggled. "You're beginning to sound like a Texan!"

"That wouldn't be so bad, would it?" Derrick shot back, his tone light. His gaze caught Taylor's for a few body-tingling seconds, and she hurriedly stood. "It's time for everyone to hit their bedrolls. I need to shut down and get camp ready for the night."

"I'll help." Derrick rose to join her.

"No, that's okay—"

"I insist."

Taylor didn't bother to argue. It had been a long, emotional day. The sooner they were cleaned up, the sooner she could zip herself into her own tent and insulated sleeping bag. The Graystones said their good nights and departed to their tent, and Taylor and Derrick made the camp ready for the evening. The mournful cry of a coyote sailed miles beyond the trees.

Derrick looked her way. "He sure sounds lonesome."

"Wait." Taylor turned from the low fire and held up her hand to listen, satisfied when another howl came from a different direction.

Derrick grinned. "His girlfriend calling him to come see her?"

"Nope. His wife chastising him for staying out too late."

Derrick laughed softly, the sound burying itself deep inside Taylor's heart. He moved closer, until the orange glow from the flames bathed his face. "I really enjoyed today, Taylor. And tonight. With you."

She sought for a witty comment but couldn't find one. Nor could she break away from the tenderness in his eyes.

"Taylor?" he asked quietly. His hand moved to brush the side of her head and the curls now hanging loose. He fingered them as though they were threads of the most delicate gold, fit only for royalty. He stared a moment longer, his eyes as dark as obsidian shimmering in the night. Then he slowly lowered his mouth to hers.

*Warm, velvet, intoxicating. . .* The words to describe his kiss shot through Taylor's mind. He wrapped his arms around her, and rational thought fled as she melted into his embrace.

A coyote's howl coming from closer than before broke them apart. They stared at one another a moment before Taylor stepped away from his arms and moved to put out the fire.

"Are we safe here?" Derrick asked.

Safe? That depended on what he was referring to. Right now, coyotes were the least of her worries. "Sure. The tents have zippers, and the food is securely stashed away." Once she finished with the fire, only scant moonlight touched them. She shoved her bare hands into fur-lined pockets. "I guess it's time to turn in. I'll see you in the morning."

"Good night, Taylor," he said as she walked off. "Sleep well."

Safely inside her tent, Taylor stripped down to a comfortable two layers and snuggled deep inside her thick sleeping bag. She reached for a thermos of hot chocolate she'd brought with her, but took only a few sips for warmth before she screwed the cap back on and lay down.

Why had she let Derrick kiss her? And why had she kissed him back? Had she lost all the good sense God gave her? That was easy to do when Derrick was near, when the warmth of his touch and his mouth played a melody on her heart. But it wasn't wise. He would be leaving in less than a week. And Taylor was no longer counting the hours until he would go.

# Chapter 4

"Hey, Taylor—wake up!"

At the sound of an excited child's voice, Taylor groggily came to. Feeling the chill bite her face, she burrowed deeper into her warm sleeping bag and tried to go back to sleep.

"Taylor, come out and see!"

The summons came again, followed by a raspy knock on the stiff tent cloth, and she held back a groan, remembering where she was. "Okay, okay, I'm coming." She made quick work of putting on her other layers of clothing, jumping up and down a little in the freezing-cold air, pulled on her boots over her thick socks, and followed it with her jacket and hat. Unzipping the tent, she stepped outside. Her eyes widened, and she lifted her gaze to the pearl gray sky, gasping in delight.

Numerous white flakes drifted gently down to touch the brown earth. A few caught Taylor on the cheeks and nose, and she giggled at their icy kiss.

"Another thing I didn't expect to see in this part of Texas," Derrick said from nearby. "Snow."

She grinned at him. "Oh, we get our share, sometimes. Several inches anyway. But I can't remember ever getting any this close to Christmas." She pocketed her hands and closed her eyes in enjoyment, her face still positioned toward the sky. "It feels like a real white Christmas now, though it'll probably melt by tomorrow. If it sticks at all."

"It's starting to stick in some places," Joshua pointed out excitedly.

"Try shoveling feet of the stuff off your sidewalk every winter," Derrick cut in. "You'd get tired of it soon enough. When I get home, I imagine I'll have a few feet to plow through just to reach the steps of my apartment building. My landlord is a couch potato and doesn't always take care of things like that."

Taylor eyed him. His words were spoken in jest, but it further reminded her that they lived in two different worlds. And Derrick was going home to his in three days.

She moved toward the camp stove. "I'll get the coffee on and heat the rest of the stew. Then we'll break camp."

Once they'd eaten a hot breakfast and cleaned up,

they left the campsite. The tents remained, since her brothers had told Taylor they'd see to taking them down. With the unexpected weather situation, Taylor felt relieved about that. She wanted to get everyone back to the ranch house as soon as possible. Blizzard-type conditions hit once in a rare moon, but it could get messy and turn to sleet.

Ten minutes into the ride, Brandon called out to Taylor, "What's that green stuff in those branches up there?"

She turned her head to look at where he pointed. "Mistletoe," she yelled back.

"You mean the Christmas-kissy stuff?" Joshua piped up.

Taylor chuckled. "Yeah."

"Let's get some," Brandon called out.

"Why would you want some old kissy-stuff?" his brother asked, clearly disgusted.

"For Granny and Gramps's anniversary," Brandon shot back. "They said they met at a Christmas dance and kissed under the mistletoe for the first time. So can we get some?"

Taylor studied the nearest tree and the moss-colored, white-berried clump hanging from its second branch. "It's not all that high, but I'm not doing any climbing. Sorry. And I didn't bring a rifle to shoot it down, either."

"You mean you can shoot, too?" Derrick asked in wonder.

She grinned at him. "I was raised on a cattle ranch, remember?"

"Will you get it down for me, Dad?" Brandon begged.

"Do we really need it?" Mr. Graystone asked, doubt etched in his voice as he looked the fifteen or so feet up the tree.

"It's Christmas! And we didn't get to have any fun and cut down a pine this year since we had to come to Texas instead. I want to give Granny and Gramps a present, too, like everyone else did!"

"I'll get it for you," Derrick offered. Taylor swung her gaze his way, watching as he dismounted. Not gracefully, but at least he didn't fall.

Was he out of his mind? Judging from this last week, outdoor, sportsman-type activities weren't in his field. The poor guy could trip on strands of hay a few inches deep.

"I don't think you should try it," Taylor said.

"I'll be all right. Not far from where I live there's a place that offers rock climbing. It has an indoor rock wall over three stories high. I go there sometimes, to unwind."

Well, that explained where his muscles and fine physique came from. Though Taylor wondered how he could keep from plummeting from such a height when on his first day at the ranch he'd fallen off a horse—and that was before he was even in the saddle!

"I want to do this for the Graystones," he added. "They were nice enough to invite me to their golden wedding anniversary. I'd like to repay the gesture and do something nice for them." He tugged his suede gloves more tightly onto his fingers then grabbed the lowest branch, swinging himself up into the tree. Taylor tensed, watching as he moved higher. Visions of his broken body and her needing to gallop away on Stardust to call an ambulance came to mind. How fast could she reach the ranch for help?

"Derrick," she called out in warning. "The branches might be slick or something. Come on down."

"No, they're fine," he grunted. "Almost there."

Heart in her mouth, Taylor watched as he reached the clump of green. At least he was wearing rubber-soled hiking shoes this time, and not those slick-soled red cowboy boots. With his arm anchored around a thick limb, he tore off the plant where it had attached itself to the tree. The greenery fell, rustling through the branches, until it hit the snow-speckled earth. Brandon let out a whoop of jubilation and jumped down from his saddle. Taylor didn't breathe until Derrick reached safety. At the last limb, he lost his grip and fell. His feet went out from under him as his shoes hit the ground.

Taylor quickly dismounted and ran his way, dropping to her hands and knees beside him. "Are you all right?" she demanded.

"Sure. I'm tough, remember? Just got the wind knocked out of me is all."

"That was a really stupid thing to do," Taylor couldn't resist saying. Nor could she resist the smile that crept to her face in answer to his boyish grin.

"I sure hope you took out an extra large insurance policy." She shook her head and straightened to her knees, settling her palms on her thighs. "You are the most accident-prone person I've ever met."

He chuckled and held out his hand. "Help me up?"

Taylor nodded and grabbed both his hands. Once he was almost on his feet, however, his heavier weight unbalanced her slighter one, and she found herself falling against his chest. His arms flew around her back. In surprise, she looked up, and their gazes locked.

"Thanks," he said.

"Sure," she whispered. Flustered, realizing the Graystones must be watching, she pushed away from him. She offered the best smile she could, though it felt feeble. "Let's get on back now. I want to get these horses some water and into a warm barn."

Taylor mounted Stardust and waited for Derrick to

do the same with Thunder. Talk about falling. . . She was doing exactly that—for Derrick. Would the impact when she hit bottom once he left the ranch shatter her heart? She was from the country; he was from the city. Both were happy with life as it was and didn't want to change. Besides, there was Kevin. A full two days had passed without her once thinking of her former fiancé. Was that wrong? After all, if it hadn't been for Taylor, Kevin would still be alive today.

❦

That evening, before the scheduled hayride, Derrick looked for Taylor in all the public rooms of the ranch house but couldn't find her.

"I saw her go to the stable earlier, while it was still light outside," Brandon offered.

Derrick thanked the boy and walked toward the wooden building. He fingered the sprig of mistletoe he'd torn from Brandon's anniversary gift to his grandparents before letting the large bough fall from the tree. Did he dare use it? The sweet kiss Derrick shared with Taylor by the campfire last night had warmed his soul and made him hungry for more. But was he pushing things too fast?

The cool wind chapped his ears. He'd left his cowboy hat in his room, but he kept walking instead of turning around to get it. He was accustomed to cold much worse than this, but he could do without the white stuff that went along with it. This morning's unexpected snowfall amounted to an accumulation of not quite three inches, and Derrick crunched through it, eyeing the pasty gray clouds that forecasted more to come in the next few hours. At least the weather prediction according to the guy on the radio was that it would warm up day after tomorrow.

Once he entered the barn, Taylor straightened from her bent position and glanced his way. Her set jaw clearly told him he was intruding. "What do you want?" she asked.

The snow outside might be melting soon, but inside things appeared as if they would remain buried in invisible frost. "The hayride is starting in a few minutes. I was hoping you might join us."

"Sorry. Can't." He could now see the wetness shimmering in her eyes. "Buttercup's sick, and I'm waiting for the vet in town to get home so he can get the message I left on his answering machine. Our regular vet is off visiting family in Missouri. I can't leave her when she's this sick."

Derrick gazed into the stall where Taylor worked. A horse Derrick remembered seeing before restlessly moved within the confined area. She let out a frantic whinny, as if in pain. Rivulets of sweat ran down the tan-colored coat as if she'd been ridden hard.

"What's wrong with her?" Derrick asked, moving closer.

"I don't know, but I suspect colic." Worried lines creased Taylor's forehead. "She's been eating her bedding, and with all the other symptoms I've seen, that's a sure sign."

"Colic—isn't that what babies get when they have too much gas?"

The look she sent his way was sober. "Yes, but in a horse it can be deadly if it's not treated soon. It can be a symptom of a bigger problem. I just wish I knew where the vet was. Robert drove into town to try to find him." She again bent down to the trough, and now Derrick could see she was removing the horse's feed.

"Anything I can do?" he asked quietly.

"I wouldn't want you to miss your hayride."

"I'd rather stay here with you and help however I can."

"Thank you." Her voice and the look she gave him this time were soft. "I have to remove all her food as long as she's like this. She needs plenty of water, though, if she'll even drink it. Take that pail and fill this other trough with it. The pump's over there."

Derrick set to work on the assigned task. Halfway through, he heard a loud crackling sound and turned to see that the horse had lowered herself to the ground and now lay on the hay. Taylor went to the mare and knelt down, stroking her long neck.

"It's okay, girl," she whispered. "We'll get you help soon. I've done all I know to do."

Sensing that Taylor was about ready to cry, Derrick finished pouring the rest of the water from the bucket into the trough then sat beside her. He took hold of her other hand, the one not stroking the horse's neck, and hoped he wasn't bungling forth where he wasn't wanted.

"Father," he said, "we turn this matter over to You. Not even a sparrow escapes Your notice, and You know how special this horse is to Taylor. We ask that You send a vet soon to save this animal, that You relieve any pain or pressure she's feeling, and give Taylor peace, in Jesus' name."

"Amen." Taylor ended the prayer. She looked at him. "Thank you. Buttercup *is* special. She's Stardust's mother, and we've had her since I was a kid. I know she's old for a horse, but I'm not ready to lose her yet."

The sorrow in her eyes suggested a deeper pain, one not yet healed. But she needed to heal. The grieving had gone on too long.

"Tell me about Kevin," Derrick said quietly.

She stiffened and pulled her hand from beneath his. Her mouth tightened and an angry spark jumped into her eyes. Maybe he was being nosy, but at least he'd gotten her mind off the present circumstances.

"Two years is a long time to hold something in, Taylor. There's a season for everything—even sorrow—but yours has gone on too long. Maybe you think I don't have any business talking about it, and I probably don't, but you need to let go of the grief. Holding on to it is a lot like not taking care of an infection. It eats away at the skin, and the wound can't heal. You have to treat the infection and get rid of it before healing can begin. Believe me, I know what I'm talking about. That's the way the counselor put it to me after my sister died. Until I talked about it and dealt with the way I felt, I didn't have much interest in continuing on with life. I wasn't suicidal or anything. I just didn't care what happened."

Her expression softened as she lifted her gaze to Derrick's. Under Taylor's gentle hand, the horse had ceased her constant fidgeting, though she jerked her body or legs from time to time. The animal seemed to rest easier now than she had when Derrick first entered the stable.

"We met at a rodeo," Taylor said at last. "Kevin was one of the spectators there, like me. We sat beside each other, started talking, and realized we had a lot of similar interests. One date led to another, and soon we were a steady item. We got engaged three months later."

Her hand stopped stroking Buttercup's neck and just lay there. She lowered her gaze to look at it. "He led me to believe he was more experienced with ranch work than he really was. When he lost his job at a pet store, I spoke up for him and got him a job here. Only he wasn't much of a cowboy, more of a show-off, really. Not in an arrogant way.

More like a big kid trying to impress."

"What happened to him?" Derrick gently prodded when she went silent.

Her face clouded. "He was working the cattle with my father and Chad. I was there, too. He hadn't had a lot of experience with roping yet, but he managed to rope a calf. He grinned up at me, proud of what he'd done. Even said, 'See, Taylor. I told you I could do it. And you didn't think I could.' That's when it happened."

She shut her eyes tight. "While he was removing the rope, his horse spooked and ran, like what happened with you the other day. His hand was still caught in the rope. He was dragged for almost a mile. When we got to him, he was almost dead." A tear slipped out from between her closed lashes. "I held him in my arms while my brother rode to get help, but he died before Chad could get back."

Derrick moved his hand to cover hers. "Taylor, I'm so sorry—"

"No!" She snatched her hand back and her eyes popped open. "Don't you dare tell me how it was just a freak accident that could've happened to anyone. I'm the one who begged Dad to give Kevin the job! Even after I saw what a mistake that was, I'm the one who encouraged Dad to keep Kevin on."

Derrick noted the flash of fire in her pale blue eyes, the remorse buried there, and understood. She blamed herself for Kevin's death. Remembering how guilt-ridden he felt after his sister was killed, Derrick held back the automatic reaction to want to respond as passionately as she did and try to convince her she wasn't to blame. Through his own experience he knew that could only make things worse. Instead he directed his gaze to the ground and the hay strewn there. He picked up a piece and began threading the yellow strand through his fingers.

"Okay, I won't tell you any of those things." He sensed her surprise in the way her body gave a little jump. "But I sure thought you had more sense than to get engaged to a guy who couldn't make a decision for himself."

Taylor bristled, like Derrick thought she would. "Kevin was very much his own man," she said, tight-lipped. "He made plenty of decisions."

"Maybe. But from what you told me, he needed you to lead him around like a horse. Even find another job for him."

"That's not true! When an opening came up at the ranch, Kevin asked me to speak to Dad about hiring him. So I did. But I thought he knew more about ranch life, as much as he talked about horses and cows."

"Hm. So what you're saying is that it was his decision to keep that information to himself, so he could land a job here. Right?"

"Yes." The word came out uncertain. She drew her

brows together as if he'd presented her with an unexpected set of equations and she didn't know the answer. "But when I found out he was inexperienced, I should have told Dad to let him go."

"That would have been hard on a relationship," Derrick mused. "I can see why you didn't. Also, it seems to me that your dad is one smart guy. Smart enough to have seen Kevin's inexperience and judge whether to let him go. Without your say in the matter."

She rubbed the space between her brows with three fingers. "I don't know. Maybe."

"Just how does one get experience at ranch life? Don't they have to live it, firsthand?"

"You're confusing me, Derrick."

"Sorry. I'm just trying to get you to think about something you've obviously never considered."

"And what's that?"

"Kevin was an adult, capable of making his own choices. If he wanted something badly enough, he sounded like the type to go after it. You couldn't have stopped him."

She fidgeted, moving her upper body in a slight turn, as though to crack her back. She looked uncomfortable, both physically and emotionally. It was time to drop the subject. He'd given her enough to consider.

"You look tired," he said. "I may not be as soft as a

pillow, but I'm here if you'd like to lean against me while we wait."

Taylor hesitated at least half a minute, then nodded and rested her back against his shoulder. She smelled like a mixture of hay and fresh flowers. Bracing one hand on the floor, Derrick slung his other arm around her, to help keep her in place. He dipped his head to inhale the clean scent of her hair, deciding it smelled like the lilac candles his mother favored. Soft strands of her curls brushed against his cheek. For a wild moment, Derrick thought about unearthing the mistletoe sprig from his pocket, but now wasn't a good time. He didn't want to take advantage of her with a surprise kiss when she was so vulnerable.

The horse gave another painful whinny and moved her head as though to rise, but quickly laid it back down. Derrick felt Taylor tense.

"Favorite Christmas carol," he said, hoping to get her mind off the situation and lighten the mood.

"What?" She turned her head sideways to look at him.

"What's your favorite Christmas carol? And why?"

"Oh. 'The Holly and the Ivy,' I guess, because when I hear the song on the radio or CD, a bunch of angelic-sounding kids are usually singing it. Children's voices are so sweet, and the carol has such an old-world English sound. Have you ever heard it?"

"Only last night at the campfire when you sang it."

He wouldn't mind owning a compilation of Taylor singing carols and strumming her guitar. "Favorite Christmas movie?"

"Is this a game?"

"You could say that. When I was a boy, Mom and I used to play this and other games like it when we were driving long distances to visit relatives over the holidays. It helped to pass the time."

"As long as you don't count any wrong answers."

He chuckled. "No counting in this game. Or wrong answers. It's a way to get to know you and what you like."

"Okay, then. *Miracle in the Wilderness*. Because it was set in the 1800s with pioneers and Native Americans. And the Christmas story of Christ's birth was told and later expressed in a way they could understand. I especially liked that."

"Favorite Christmas book?"

"Except for my Bible, I don't get a lot of reading in. Mom belongs to an inspirational romance club that sent her some Christmas-themed books that look pretty interesting. I might try to read one or two of those in the coming weeks."

"What about your favorite Christmas kids' show?"

"That's easy. The Charlie Brown one."

"Why?"

"I loved it when Linus recited the passage of Jesus'

birth from the Bible, then later the kids all helped Charlie Brown feel better about his sad choice of a tree."

"Christmas song from a movie?"

" 'I'll Be Home for Christmas'—because I like Judy Garland and her movies." She paused. "I don't hear you telling me any of yours."

He chuckled. "Okay. 'Jingle Bells' for a favorite carol—because I always got to ring the handbells when we went caroling. Mom headed the group. She was the church choir director, and I was the youngest kid there. She couldn't afford a sitter in those days, so I always got dragged around with her." He grinned at the memory. He loved his mom and all she'd sacrificed for him. He hoped her new marriage made her happy.

"What else?" Taylor prodded.

"For a Christmas movie—*It's a Wonderful Life*, because I rooted for the guy all the way through and was glad when he asked God to get him back home. Christmas book—I've only read *A Christmas Carol*, and that was long ago. It was required reading for school, but it held my interest, and I liked the way it ended. Kids' show—*The Grinch*, 'cause he was such a crusty old guy but had a good heart underneath it all. He saved his dog."

She looked sideways at him again, and he gave her a big smile.

"You're a pretty nice guy yourself," she admitted.

"Thanks." He lifted his eyebrows in amused surprise at the compliment. "But I hope that doesn't mean you think me crusty or old."

Pink stained her cheeks, and she turned her head back around. "What have you learned about me? Or dare I even ask?"

"Sure. You're a sweet, down-home girl who enjoys the simple pleasures of life. You have a strong faith in God and a sensitive heart. And I'll bet you even cried when Charlie Brown saw the decked-out tree and all those kids yelled, 'Merry Christmas, Charlie Brown!' "

"Did not." The grin lifting her lips said otherwise. "Well, maybe a little."

He chuckled and hugged her closer to him for a moment. If not for the horse's condition, this would be perfect. The soft yellow glow of the inside lights, the warmth of her pressed against him. . . Cozy. Something he could definitely get used to.

"Now it's your turn to be rated," she said, interrupting his train of thought. "Judging from what you said, I think you're a guy who wants everyone everywhere to overcome their problems, especially those people whom others give up on. You see the good in everyone, so you want all to succeed, and you do what you can to help, even if it means just rooting for people."

"Not a bad analysis," he mused. "But I'm not sure I'm as golden-hearted as that. With all the trouble at my new job, I'm about ready to quit from the stress."

"Trouble?"

"Someone's been mismanaging the accounts at the firm I work for. Probably the former accountant, though I'm just assuming. An investigation is under way now. I'm exempt from being suspect, because I was hired a little over a month ago. But soon I'll have to go back into the ugly corporate jungle."

Taylor stiffened against him. "In three days."

"Yeah." Derrick grew somber. He didn't want to leave but had no choice. If the situation went to trial, he might have to testify. He wished he could take Taylor with him to Chicago.

The sudden thought surprised him.

Even if their relationship did progress to something bigger, he could never ask her to leave the ranch she loved. She belonged here, and instinctively Derrick knew she would wither up in a huge congested city, with no horse to ride over the vast, empty land, or campouts in the middle of the peaceful woods. She was every inch a country girl. He couldn't change that—nor did he want to.

A movement at the stable door alerted them both to company. Robert strode in, followed by a squat, middle-aged man wearing gray slacks and a white dress shirt under his long, unbuttoned trench coat. A black satchel was in his hand.

Robert lifted his brow upon nearing the stall and seeing Taylor snug against Derrick. She quickly leaned forward and scrambled to her feet. "You're the vet?" she asked, walking toward the newcomer.

"Yes, ma'am. Howard Feldman's the name. It's a good thing your brother found me when he did. Me and my wife were just fixing to head on over to her parents' place in the next county. Now, what have we here?" He approached Buttercup, and Derrick rose from his sitting position.

"I'll go back to the house now and get out of your way," he said.

Taylor offered him a faint smile. "Thanks for keeping me company."

As Derrick retraced the shallow impressions his footsteps had made in the snow, he wondered about the cheerless look in her eyes. Was it only concern for her horse? Or had something else been said to make her look like her world was nearing the brink of collapse?

# Chapter 5

After an enormous Christmas dinner featuring barbecued roast beef, buttery mashed potatoes, onion-flavored green beans, corn on the cob, and much more, Derrick joined the Summeralls in the family room. Taylor passed out the gifts that had mysteriously accumulated under the tree this past week, and Derrick was surprised when she handed him a thin, square-shaped one. His brows lifted.

"You shouldn't have, Taylor."

"Oh, it's not from me," she hastened to say. "It's from the family, though Chad picked it out."

Derrick nodded his friend's way and opened the shiny blue wrap. Pleasure shot through him when he saw a CD of gospel hymns with Taylor's smiling face on the cover.

Taylor pierced her brother with a glare. "He's right,

Chad. You really shouldn't have."

"Oh, lighten up, Taylor," Robert said with a grin.

Derrick looked from Chad to Taylor then back again. "But how. . . ?"

"Yesterday you told me how much you enjoyed Taylor's singing," Chad explained. "And I remembered that she'd done that years ago. A friend of Dad's is a local radio DJ—he's the one we listen to every night—and in exchange for him staying here with his family one weekend, he got permission to let us borrow the studio to make that. It was during her senior year in high school, if I remember right."

Derrick looked at the picture on the cover again. Taylor's eyes sparkled with a childlike innocence and glow, as if nothing in her world had ever gone wrong. Obviously the photo was taken before Kevin's accident. "This is great! Thanks. I can't wait to pop it into my player at home."

"And thank you," Charla Summerall said from across the room, an unwrapped box in her lap. "We always do love these sausage and cheese sets. I can't wait to try them all."

Derrick smiled then noticed that Taylor had picked up his present to her, shaped exactly as his gift had been. From her place on the sofa, she shot him an uncertain look.

"It won't bite," he said with a grin.

Pink flushed her cheeks, but she slid her short nail

under the flap and opened it. "Oh, Derrick. . ." She smiled up at him. "The best of Judy Garland. Thank you."

Derrick was glad he'd agreed to go Christmas shopping with Chad yesterday and had found that CD. Yet before he could answer her, Lou Summerall stood and faced his wife. A commanding figure who towered well over six feet, with graying hair and swarthy skin, Lou was the type of man to capture the attention of a roomful of people.

"And now for your gift, Charla darlin'."

"Oh, but. . ." She touched the diamond drop necklace around her neck. "Isn't this it?"

Lou chuckled. "That's just from me. But this next gift is from your sons, too. Now, close your eyes."

"This is all so mysterious," she drawled.

Derrick heard Taylor gasp and turned to look. Chad and Will carried what appeared to be a big, varnished oak cabinet and set it in front of their mother.

"You can open your eyes now," Lou prodded.

She did so and squealed. "Oh—how beautiful! Will, you must've been the one to burn those scrolls into the wood. They look just like something you did when you were a boy in wood shop. But. . .where will I put it? It doesn't have any legs."

At this, all three of her sons laughed. Lou bent down and said quietly, "It's not supposed to have any legs. It's for the kitchen we're going to remodel for you, the one you've been begging me to do for years? This is just one of the cabinets. There are five more like it out in the shed. And new drawers, too."

"Oh, Lou!" She threw her arms around her husband, almost pulling him down to her lap with the exuberance of her hug, then just as suddenly she released him and jumped up. "And I know just where they'll go, too. Come along with me, all of you. This is so wonderful—you're all so wonderful—I can't wait!" She hurried from the room.

Shaking their heads and smiling, the Summerall men followed. Before Taylor could rise to join them, Derrick spoke. "You have one more present."

She wrinkled her brow and looked in the immediate area around her. "Are you sure?"

"Yes." He rose from his chair and walked across the room to take a seat beside her on the sofa. "I'm glad to hear Buttercup's doing better."

Taylor searched the discarded gift wrap around her feet. "She's able to eat again. I'm so thankful she got through this crisis and we were able to find a skilled vet."

She located the rectangular-shaped box in the same style of glossy green paper that Derrick had used to wrap the CD. This time when she opened her gift, she laughed. "*A Charlie Brown Christmas*! Oh, how perfect, Derrick. Thank you."

"We can cuddle up on the couch and watch it to-night, after the others go to bed."

At his low words, she seemed suddenly hesitant. "Are you trying to tell me that you're interested in me?"

"Would you mind very much if I was?"

"No, I don't think so. But what would be the point? You're leaving for Chicago tomorrow—"

He shook his head slightly, lifting his fingers to barely touch her lips when she opened her mouth to say more. "Let's take this one step at a time," he suggested, pulling his other hand from his pants pocket.

"What's that you have there?"

He held up the tiny sprig of mistletoe for her inspection. This time her whole face turned pink, but she didn't pull away. That fact encouraged him.

"In keeping with the Christmas tradition," he murmured, raising it above her head. He slowly drew closer, watching her beautiful blue eyes dilate. . .and close. Then he shut his own eyes and tenderly kissed her.

Later, in her room, Taylor stood at her window with its view of the side lawn and stared at the red luminaries glowing in the dark. She couldn't believe she'd let Derrick kiss her a second time. Worse, she'd kissed him back. . . and liked it. Then an hour ago they'd sat side by side on the couch, eating soft pralines and watching the Peanuts gang learn the true meaning of Christmas. She couldn't remember a more enjoyable time, unless she counted the other night, by the campfire. . .

The muted ring of her bedside phone caught her attention, and she moved to grab it on the third ring, taking note of the steady yellow glow of one of the buttons. An inside call. No doubt Chad was calling to apologize for something.

"Hello?"

"I hope I didn't wake you."

Her heart began a funny cadence as warmth rushed to her face. "Derrick. No—I. . ." She fought for control. He probably needed towels or something. She couldn't remember if she'd stocked his room with enough of them. "I hope there's not a problem?"

"No. I just wanted to hear your voice."

The tingling warmth shot down through her fingers and toes, but she couldn't think of anything to say.

"I've enjoyed my stay here with your family. And tonight, with you," his low voice caressed her ear several seconds later.

"I'm glad. You're welcome to come visit us again anytime." She winced when she realized how professional she sounded.

"Is that a personal invitation?"

How to answer that? "Um. . .sure."

A longer pause ensued. "By the way, those pralines were delicious. Chad told me you made them."

"Yes. I'll have Mom box some up for you for your plane trip, if you'd like." There. She'd said it. He was going. The reminder put the starch back into her bones. How could he play with her emotions like this, when he knew how it might hurt her?

"I'll miss you, Taylor."

Her eyes slid shut, and she swallowed hard. "Yeah," she whispered.

"Are you all right? You sound upset."

"I'm just tired. I'll see you in the morning at breakfast."

"Okay." He sounded disappointed. "Good night."

Frowning, Taylor hung up the phone and went to the bathroom sink. Bending over, she rinsed the sting from her eyes with cold water. The phone rang again.

She was there on the second ring.

"Hi," she said breathlessly into the receiver. "I'm sorry I was so hard to talk to a minute ago—"

"Taylor?" Chad asked. "What are you talking about?"

Her heart did a little nosedive. "Oh, hi, Chad. Nothing. That was a wonderful present you guys gave Mom. I haven't seen her face light up like that in a long time."

"Then I'm forgiven?"

Taylor couldn't help the small grin that lifted her lips. She blotted her damp face with the hand towel she'd grabbed before sprinting from the bathroom. "For what this time?"

"For pairing you off with Derrick and asking you to keep him company these past ten days."

Her amusement evaporated, and she focused on the lavender lamp shade.

"I noticed that you seemed to be getting along pretty well with each other today. So maybe it wasn't all a complete waste of your time?"

"No, it was fine." She tossed the towel onto the bed and bent over to pull the blankets down.

"Did you know that Dad offered Derrick a job managing the books?"

She froze in shock, then snapped to a stand. "No, I didn't. What did he say?"

"He thanked Dad but said he had to get back to Chicago."

Of course. He must miss the big city life.

"Are you there?"

"Yeah. Listen, I'm pretty tired. I think I'll turn in now."

"Okay. I just wanted to call and assure you that I had your best interests in mind from the start. Maybe I came off like an uncaring jerk at the beginning, but I really do care about you, Taylor."

"I know." She smiled, and another set of tears pricked her eyes. It was a rarity for Chad to talk about his emotions, so this was a milestone. "I love you, too, big brother. Good night."

Once Taylor hung up the phone, she finished getting ready for bed then slid between the cold sheets. She curled her body around a pillow she held in an effort to warm up. Tomorrow Derrick would be gone, and life would go on as it had before he came. Any far-reaching, misty dream she'd entertained of him staying had evaporated in the harsh light of reality. Her dad offered him the chance, and he'd turned it down. Flat. Derrick belonged in the city. Yet, at this moment, Taylor felt he would take her heart with him when he went.

# *Chapter 6*

Derrick stood at the window of his fifth-floor apartment and studied the bustling city below. Lights from building windows and cars pierced the darkness of the evening sky. Now and then a horn would honk from the direction of a street still under repairs, shattering the relative stillness. A fresh snow was falling, but it would soon turn the sooty gray of what was already on the ground. That's one thing he liked about Texas. The snow stayed white, probably because it melted within a matter of days, and there hadn't been such a heavy accumulation that shoveling was necessary. In fact, the white stuff hadn't been much of a bother at all.

In the background, Taylor's clear, sweet voice sang to him from his stereo speakers. He had played the CD almost nonstop since his return home. It was almost as good as having her there with him. He'd never missed a person so much, and only three days had passed since he left the ranch. How could a girl he'd known for such a short time affect him so strongly?

*Because you're in love with her,* his mind whispered back.

Derrick pulled away from the window and surveyed the empty, stark room decorated in brass, black, and dim white. It was true. He loved the short, sassy cowgirl, and Chad probably knew it, too. Why else, at the airport, would he have kept introducing the subject of Taylor? Chad's questions about their time together had been off-hand, but frequent enough for him to realize that his buddy suspected Derrick's feelings ran deep.

He missed Taylor horribly.

A burning smell invaded his nostrils and made Derrick grimace. *Oh, no. I must've forgotten to set the timer.*

He rushed into his compact kitchen, pulled on the checkered mitts, and withdrew his charred pre-made lasagna dinner from the oven. Smoke swept upward, setting off the smoke alarm. A shrill blare penetrated the area and he felt as if his eardrums might burst. Leaving the cardboard tray of burnt food on the rack, he shed his mitts and disengaged the alarm.

The sudden quiet brought welcome relief, though it seemed invasive, too. After such a din, the silence gave the impression of being underlined, and Derrick felt even more alone, especially since the last track on the CD had ended.

He took a fork and removed the top layer of burnt cheese from his dinner, glad to see that the noodles, meat, and red sauce underneath looked okay to eat. Still, even unburned, this meal couldn't compare to the homemade meals that Taylor's mom served at the ranch.

The phone rang, and Derrick grabbed it, thankful to whoever was on the other end. He needed someone to talk to right now to save him from his blue-without-you thoughts. "Hello?"

"Derrick," his boss said. "Sorry to call so late, but this is important."

"Not a problem." Derrick leaned against the counter. "I'm listening."

Five minutes later he hung up the receiver, feeling stunned.

Was this God's hand at work?

❧

Taylor reclined on the couch, with her head against a round pillow cushion, and took advantage of the down-time to read the last chapter of her mother's Christmas-themed suspense book. Who would have thought a Christian romance could have such an impact on her life? All of the many different methods God used to encourage His people amazed her.

Like the heroine in the book who was upset about a brother on trial for murder, Taylor blamed herself for a loved one's choices. She'd felt responsible for Kevin's death because she'd gotten him the job at the ranch. Yet, Derrick was right. Kevin had made his own choices, and regardless of what Taylor might have said or done otherwise, he would have acted as he wanted. God didn't hold her responsible for what had happened to Kevin. Taylor had been the one to slap on her own self-made handcuffs and fasten them tightly around her wrists.

While reading the novel these past few days, she'd been led to put down the book at times and search out scriptures mentioned in the story. Portions that enlightened the heroine to the truth, as well as other verses. God's promises from the verses of Jeremiah especially helped Taylor:

" 'For I know the plans I have for you,' declares the Lord, 'plans to prosper you and not to harm you, plans to give you hope and a future. Then you will call upon me and come and pray to me, and I will listen to you. You will seek me and find me when you seek me with all your heart.' "

Taylor had been doing exactly that, especially over her feelings concerning Derrick. She'd thought about him for almost a week, ever since the day he left, and she'd come to the knowledge that it was all right for her to love again—that God desired to give her a future, one filled with hope. Was that future with Derrick?

Chad had Derrick's phone number. Maybe in the new year she would break down and give him a call. If things between them were meant to progress, they would. Long distance and differing lifestyles didn't matter if she and Derrick were supposed to be together. She'd been pouring her heart out to God for almost a week now, and she was convinced that He'd heard her. Whatever happened, His plans for her were best.

Taylor finished the story, which ended in a cozy-warm way to make her feel good inside. She put the book down and stretched, then sank back against the cushion. The heroine had ended up making the decision to move to the hero's state to share his life, and Taylor's mind wandered back to Derrick. What if they did start seeing each other and their relationship matured to such a point that God told her to move to Chicago? Could she do that?

She thought about the fresh country air, riding Stardust, and the acres and acres of empty, wild, beautiful land on which she lived. It would be difficult to leave the home she loved behind, but there was such a thing as visits. And the twenty-first century did make it easy to cover a thousand miles or more. Her time with the Lord this past week had helped Taylor understand that if God were behind a possible move on her part, she wouldn't be happy doing otherwise. Yet He'd have to make the directive very clear to her for her to do such a thing as leave Texas.

Taylor's face warmed. Here she was planning out their married life together, when she and Derrick had never even been out on an official date!

"Hey, there you are."

Chad's loud voice interrupted her thoughts, and she shot to a sitting position. She felt embarrassed that she'd been dreaming like a silly schoolgirl who'd linked her and her boyfriend's names in a hand-drawn heart. Good thing no one could read her thoughts!

"Don't tell me you haven't got any plans for New Year's Eve?" Chad asked, his gaze taking in her rumpled sweatshirt and jeans. He was spruced up in a nice pair of black slacks and a patterned sweater.

"I thought I'd just stay home and watch the ball in New York come down on TV. Besides, if the Masons want anything, with Dad and Mom gone to the dance, and you and Robert and Will all on dates, someone has to stay behind and keep things running."

"The Masons are on their honeymoon," Chad argued with a grin. "I doubt you'll be getting any phone calls from their room."

"Maybe not, but I'd rather stay home tonight. I might even start another one of these novels. Mom has a shelf full of them, and they're really good. Much better than I expected."

Chad feigned an expression of horror. "Oh no! Not another romance junkie in the house! Life was bad enough when it was just Mom, but now you've been bit by the bug, too?"

Taylor chuckled. "Yeah, I guess I have."

"Well, I'll quit trying to push you out of the house then. From what I've seen, there's no known cure for the romance junkie. I'll talk to you later."

"Are you bringing Karen to dinner tomorrow?"

Chad's face actually turned a shade of salmon. "I plan to. You'll like her, I think. She was raised on a ranch, too, and she's different from those 'empty-headed females' I brought home in the past. I believe that's what you called them." His tone lightened to teasing.

"I look forward to meeting her then. It's time you found a nice girl to settle down with."

"Don't rush me." He seemed nervous. "Listen, as long as you're not going anywhere, can I borrow your car? My truck's been stalling on me lately, and I wouldn't want the old girl to go temperamental while I'm with Karen."

"Sure. The keys are in my bedroom, on the bureau."

"Thanks."

Taylor chuckled and watched Chad hurry from the room. Obviously a romance bug of a different sort had bitten her brother.

With hours to while away until midnight and no

guests who needed her, Taylor enjoyed a leisurely shower, dried her hair with a blow dryer, zipped herself into a pair of faded blue jeans, and pulled on one of her softest, fluffiest sweaters. Taking her desire to pamper herself to another level, she grabbed a pint of peppermint ice cream from the freezer and a spoon from the drawer. Sock-footed, she padded back to the couch. She made herself comfortable and spooned what was left of the decadently sweet stuff into her mouth, her gaze going out the window over the decorated lawn. She crunched down on the candy pieces, thinking.

Not quite the way she'd thought she would spend New Year's Eve, but this wasn't so bad. It was better than going to the community dance alone.

Ice cream finished, a glance at the wall clock told her she still had a little more than an hour to kill before midnight. She remembered that Mom had asked her to make another batch of soft pralines for New Year's Day. Might as well take care of that now.

To keep her company, she switched on the tabletop radio in the kitchen. It was set at her dad's station, and she left the dial there, enjoying the oldies music. She had just set the cooked candy mixture aside to cool when a soft drink commercial ended and the station jingle played. The DJ's deep, fluid voice captured her attention:

"This might seem a week late to some of you folks

out there, but since the caller assures me that there really are twelve days of Christmas—and don't we have the song to prove it?—I thought I'd go ahead and play the requested tune one last time. This goes out to Taylor from Derrick."

Taylor froze, spoon in midair, her eyes going wide. Her gaze whipped to the black box on her mother's kitchen counter. From its small speaker, strains of "I'll Be Home for Christmas" floated through the kitchen. The singer wasn't Judy Garland, but even if it had been the Abominable Snowman, Taylor probably wouldn't have known the difference. She stood, disbelieving, her mouth open.

Surely the DJ meant another Taylor and Derrick. It had to be one of those strange-but-true coincidences. Their names weren't all that common, but this sort of thing happened occasionally, didn't it? What other explanation could there be? Derrick wouldn't be calling from Chicago to request a song.

Her heart calmed to a steadier beat. She retrieved the pecan halves from the cabinet and had just sprinkled a few into a measuring cup when the DJ came on the air again.

"Well, there you have it. Since I know this little lady personally, I agreed to deliver a message along with the song. Taylor, if you're out there and are listening—you get yourself off that ranch and on down to the bus station on McGregor Street as quick as you can. Derrick will be outside waiting for you."

Taylor dropped the one-pound bag, and pecans scattered all over the tiles.

⁓

Derrick cast a nervous smile toward the crowd who'd gathered, then glanced at his wristwatch again. What if she didn't show? Maybe it had been a mistake to call the DJ and have the man relay his message to Taylor. Ever since the song aired, curious people had trickled into the bus depot like those in New York Times Square who'd eagerly waited for the ball to drop an hour ago. Cars drove up and parked, some keeping watch inside, while others joined Derrick and took a spot on the sidewalk that stretched in front of the cement building. Derrick quit counting the onlookers when he reached fifty-five. Honestly! Didn't these people have anything better to do on New Year's Eve than to stand outside a bus depot?

Derrick didn't want to think about the possibility of Taylor not making an appearance, but the thought had darted through his mind these past thirty minutes like a persistent gnat. She might not have been listening to the radio tonight. She might have gone to a party or a dance. Why had he assumed that she'd be sitting at home anyway? Or that she'd be interested in furthering their relationship?

He should have thought this through. If he had ordered a taxi and quietly arrived at The Silver Spur, at least he would have been saved the humiliation and disappointment if she didn't show.

An elderly woman walked up to him, pulling her down coat closer around her neck. "What time do you have?" she asked, her breath misting in the air.

Derrick looked at his watch. "Fifteen 'til."

She smiled. "Chin up, young man. She'll show."

Derrick's face warmed. He wished he could be so sure.

The minutes crawled by on inchworm feet. More cars pulled up. More people got out. He wished the radio station that the Summeralls listened to wasn't as popular as it obviously was. The town was small, but apparently everyone in the vicinity who'd been listening had turned out to watch.

Suddenly, Derrick heard what sounded like horse hooves clattering over blacktop. He turned to look, as did the rest of the crowd. Taylor came riding around the corner on Stardust, her hair catching the glow of outside lights and bouncing around her shoulders.

"There she is!" an excited little girl cried out.

The crowd cheered. As Taylor drew close, Derrick saw the disbelief that made her eyes go round when she noticed the two long lines of smiling faces and those who craned their heads from the windows of their cars. Her face was flushed, whether from the ride or from embarrassment, Derrick didn't know. If she felt like he did, it was probably a little of both.

He moved forward, almost stumbling over his own feet in his eagerness to be with her. She spotted him, and her expression relaxed as she gave him one of the biggest smiles he'd ever seen. In a matter of seconds, they reached each other. Taylor dismounted, a bystander took the reins, and she moved into Derrick's arms. Another cheer went up.

"It's so good to hold you again," Derrick murmured in her ear, lifting her off the ground. He laid his cheek against her soft, sweet-smelling hair. After a few seconds passed, he reluctantly loosed his tight hold and set her back on her feet. Near to bursting with his news and unable to contain it any longer, he blurted, "I'm out of a job!"

She drew her brows together in confusion. "You sound happy about it."

"I am. The firm's gone bankrupt, though I'm sorry for those involved. I don't have to testify in court, either. They caught the embezzler, and word has it that he'll plea-bargain to get a lighter sentence."

Her brow creased as if she were desperately trying to figure out his words.

He laughed. "Taylor, I have nothing to keep me in

Chicago anymore! If your dad still has that position for a personal accountant open, I'd like to take it. I've found I really like Texas. Especially the people here." His hands moved to cradle her chilled face. "And I love you."

"Really, Derrick?" Her eyes shone.

"Yes. I couldn't stop thinking about you all this past week. I want to spend as much time as I can getting to know you, getting to know everything about you."

"I'd like that," she said shyly. "Because I think I love you, too."

Though it was thirty-two degrees, the admission warmed him clear through. He studied every inch of her face, every curve, every freckle. His gaze lifted to her shimmering blue one and locked.

"What are you thinking?" she whispered.

"I'm just counting the stars in your eyes."

She grinned and wrapped her arms around him. "Be quiet and kiss me, city boy."

"With pleasure." He dipped his head and touched his lips to her soft ones. They were icy-cold and he quickly warmed them, enjoying the desirable task.

Car horns began to honk. Party whistles and blowers blew. Stardust whinnied.

"Happy New Year!" someone shouted from nearby.

Derrick broke the kiss, his face only inches from Taylor's.

"Happy New Year," she whispered.

He smiled. "Happy New Year." Bending down, he reclaimed her lips until Stardust's loud whinny broke them apart a second time.

"We'd better get out of here," Taylor said, giggling, "before we have to chase another runaway horse. Stardust is more stable than the others, but I don't want to take any chances. I'll give you a ride back to the ranch. One of the boys can come and pick up your luggage later. I assume you left it inside?"

Derrick nodded, and she mounted and reclaimed the reins while he awkwardly swung up behind her. He wrapped his arms around her waist. "This'll be a great year, Taylor, for both of us. It's a brand-new start, the best year yet."

Taylor smiled and settled back against his chest for the ride home.

# Epilogue

*One year later*

T hey're coming!"

The excited squeal from outside met Taylor's ears, and automatically she covered her styled-for-the-occasion hair with her free hand. She walked quickly past numerous pots of red and white poinsettias placed on the edge of the stairs, and rows of sweet-smelling pine garland that draped the walls. Her other hand she kept firmly wrapped around Derrick's.

Before they could make it to the sunny outdoors, he stopped her at the door.

"What?" she asked, wondering if they'd forgotten something. Their luggage was at the bus station being guarded by Robert and Will.

Derrick pointedly looked at the mistletoe hanging above their heads, and Taylor grinned. He bent his head toward her. His kiss took her breath away, even if it was brief.

"You ready for this?" he asked, eyes twinkling.

She matched his smile. "Ready when you are."

He opened the door, and together they raced outside, trying in vain to cover their heads while showers of heart-shaped rice rained down on them from the guests lined up along the steps and sidewalk of the ranch house. They both laughed as they ran toward Stardust, saddled and waiting for the short ride that would take Taylor and her new husband to the depot, where they would catch a bus for the airport, then be on their way to a honeymoon cruise in the Caribbean. Chad held Stardust's reins to keep him steady, and Karen looped her arm through his, her new engagement ring catching flashes of light.

Taylor took a moment to hug the woman who'd become such a good friend. "I'm so glad you're going to be my sister." She looked toward her brother. "Thanks, Chad. For everything. And yes, you're definitely forgiven."

She chuckled at the confusion that crossed his face, and gave him a quick hug, too. Then she hugged her parents. Her mom whispered in her ear, "What was that all about?"

"Chad forced me to give lessons to Derrick when he

first came here a year ago," Taylor explained before she moved away.

"Ah," her mom said, a twinkle in her eye. "Then, I'm glad he did. I've never seen you so happy."

"Welcome to the family, Taylor," Derrick's mom said, wrapping Taylor and Derrick in a close hug. "You both have a wonderful life together. And believe me, you'll love the cruise."

A group of Taylor's small cousins moved in and began throwing handfuls of rice at close range.

"We'd better get out of here." Taylor laughed. "I'll call you when we reach the hotel, Mom. See y'all in two weeks."

Derrick mounted the gelding with expertise. His past year on the ranch had served him well, riding with Taylor almost every day. Her city boy was now a fine horseman. He held out one hand to her and helped to pull her up on the saddle. She was glad she'd worn her gray wool slacks, fuzzy white top, and gray snakeskin boots. Her mother's suggestion of a blouse with a full skirt for a going-away outfit would never have worked in this chilly December weather. Even with her thermals and new down jacket she felt cold, and she wrapped her arms tightly around Derrick's middle.

"Mm," he said with a backward smile her way. "That's nice. You can do that anytime you'd like, Mrs. Freeborn."

Smiling, she snuggled closer. *Mrs. Freeborn*. She could hear that name from sunup to sundown and never get tired of it.

"Are you ready to ride off into the sunset together?" he asked.

She raised her brows at the corny line. "Only if you don't stop to count the cows."

He laughed, a pleasant, rich sound that shook the air. Taylor knew she'd never grow tired of that laugh, either. Nor of his infectious smile.

They waved their good-byes to family and friends who'd come to share in the joy of their Christmas wedding. Then Derrick prodded Stardust into a gallop, and they rode across the wide land together. Ahead of them, the magnificent red ball of the sun dipped beyond the horizon and tinted the clouds with mellow rose and violet. The guests' parting calls of good wishes became a pleasant background murmur in Taylor's ears. Smiling, she laid her cheek against the suede material covering Derrick's broad back. She had hope again, and the assurance of a bright future with this wonderful man who possessed a heart as big as Texas.

God's promises really did come true.

# TAYLOR'S SOFT PRALINES
## (Ultra-rich, ultra sweet, ultra creamy)

¾ cup milk
2 cups sugar + 1 cup sugar
1¾ cups pecan halves or peanuts
1 tsp. vanilla

Over low heat, cook milk and 2 cups sugar in 4-quart saucepan, stirring frequently. Meanwhile, caramelize 1 cup sugar in skillet over low heat, achieving a syrupy, golden brown appearance, and stirring as needed so sugar doesn't burn. Add to milk mixture. Cook to soft ball stage, stirring all the while. Cool until lukewarm. Add vanilla and nuts. Beat until creamy and spread thickly on waxed paper. Break apart into pieces when dry.

Enjoy!

**Pamela Griffin** lives in North Central Texas and divides her time among God, family, and writing. Her main goal in writing Christian fiction is to encourage others and plant seeds of faith through entertaining stories that minister to the wounded spirit. Christmas is her favorite time of year, and she enjoys writing stories centered on the season. She has contracted over twenty novels and novellas and loves hearing from her readers. You can visit her at: http://users.waymark.net/words_of_honey/.

# A Letter to Our Readers

Dear Readers:

In order that we might better contribute to your reading enjoyment, we would appreciate your taking a few minutes to respond to the following questions. When completed, please return to the following: Fiction Editor, Barbour Publishing, Inc., P.O. Box 719, Uhrichsville, OH 44683.

1. Did you enjoy reading *Room at the Inn*?
   □ Very much—I would like to see more books like this.
   □ Moderately—I would have enjoyed it more if _____
   _____
   _____

2. What influenced your decision to purchase this book?
   (Check those that apply.)
   □ Cover          □ Back cover copy          □ Title          □ Price
   □ Friends        □ Publicity                □ Other

3. Which story was your favorite?
   □ *Orange Blossom Christmas*     □ *Mustangs and Mistletoe*

4. Please check your age range:
   □ Under 18          □ 18–24          □ 25–34
   □ 35–45             □ 46–55          □ Over 55

5. How many hours per week do you read? _____

Name _____

Occupation _____

Address _____

City _____ State _____ Zip _____

E-mail _____

# If you enjoyed

# *ROOM AT THE INN*

## then read:

# ALL JINGLED OUT

*TWO SWEET AND LIGHT TALES OF "MOM INGENUITY" IN THE WAKE OF HOLIDAY MAYHEM*

*All Done with the Dashing* by Pamela Dowd
*My True Love Gave to Me* by Christine Lynxwiler

If you enjoyed

# *ROOM AT THE INN*

### then read:

# KEEPING CHRISTMAS

*Two Stories*
*Two solitary lives*
*One season of change*

Two Stories by Wanda Luttrell

*No Holly, No Ivy*
*O Little Town of Progress*

# $\mathcal{H}$EARTSONG ❤ PRESENTS

# Love Stories Are Rated G!

That's for godly, gratifying, and of course, great! If you love a thrilling love story but don't appreciate the sordidness of some popular paperback romances, **Heartsong Presents** is for you. In fact, **Heartsong Presents** is the premiere inspirational romance book club featuring love stories where Christian faith is the primary ingredient in a marriage relationship.

Sign up today to receive your first set of four, never-before-published Christian romances. Send no money now; you will receive a bill with the first shipment. You may cancel at any time without obligation, and if you aren't completely satisfied with any selection, you may return the books for an immediate refund!

Imagine. . .four new romances every four weeks—two historical, two contemporary—with men and women like you who long to meet the one God has chosen as the love of their lives. . .all for the low price of $10.99 postpaid.

To join, simply complete the coupon below and mail to the address provided. **Heartsong Presents** romances are rated G for another reason: They'll arrive Godspeed!

## YES! Sign me up for Hearts❤ng!

**NEW MEMBERSHIPS WILL BE SHIPPED IMMEDIATELY!**
**Send no money now.** We'll bill you only $10.99 postpaid with your first shipment of four books. Or for faster action, call toll free 1-800-847-8270.

NAME _____

ADDRESS _____

CITY _____ STATE_____ ZIP_____

**MAIL TO: HEARTSONG PRESENTS, P.O. Box 721, Uhrichsville, Ohio 44683**
**or visit www.heartsongpresents.com**